*To my son Leonardo, with the hope
that in his life he can do
and be what makes him happiest.*

Mediosfera © 2016-2022 www.Mediosfera.it

The information contained in the following text was collected with diligence and in good faith and, where possible, scrupulously verified on multiple sources. However, if any inaccuracies are identified, please report it promptly to the e-mail address indicated below, which we invite you to use also for comments, criticisms and suggestions.

Write to Andrea Fiorini at: fiorini@mediosfera.it

HISTORY OF ONLINE TRADING

From The Origins To The Boom

Andrea Fiorini

INTRODUCTION

The convergence of finance, information technology and telecommunications

As with almost all historical phenomena, there is no starting date of online trading, a precise time of its creation. Instead, there is a long theory of events, of people, of choices, of processes started and then interrupted, resumed, and completed, which in their development have at times taken unexpected and unexpected directions.

In fact, online trading combines the experiences and skills of two main sectors: finance (the set of activities that involve transactions of capital therefore not of material assets) and telematics. A term, the latter, perhaps obsolete but very topical, given that in recent years the spread of broadband by wire and by radio has given rise to a profound interpenetration between telecommunications operators and technologies and those of the "computer science" strictu senso. A term, the latter, coined in 1962 by the scientist Philippe Dreyfus through the union of the French words *"information"* and *"automatique"* with the meaning of information processing by means of automatisms.

And "telematics" arises precisely from the merger of "information technology" and "telecommunications" (remote communications) in the sense of "automated processing of information at a distance".

Finance, information technology and telecommunications therefore met after a long journey, which began, as regards the first sector, in the 7th century BC in Anatolia with the invention of money; for the second, in the seventeenth century AD with the applications developed by Blaise Pascal and Gottfried Leibniz on the basis of philosophical reflections and technological experiments whose origin is lost in the mists of time and, in the third, in the meaning considered here, with studies on radio waves and electromagnetism at the beginning of the 19th century.

The acceleration of the development process of information technology and telematics takes place starting from the Second World War. In these years, from 1943 in particular, the military powers of Europe, America and Asia poured on the war and industrial apparatus the technological potential developed quickly, with great urgency and determination in the course of a frantic and bloody small number of years that represent a real struggle for the survival of the nations involved, in which all economic, intellectual, military and food resources are centralized and coordinated with a single purpose: to fight and prevail over the enemy. The subsequent Cold War then pushes many nations not only to continue the development of increasingly powerful and sophisticated weapons, but also of technologies and related applications that allow both to maintain military supe-riority for deterrent purposes and to spread in industry and civil society the discoveries made up to that point. In the United States, in particular, thanks to huge orders from the Department of Defense, industries are developing new patents that apply to an enormous mass of new products and materials, an activity supported by the recovery in consumption and the widespread well-being of a nation not directly affected. from the destruction of war.

If the US Defense budget hits an all-time high of 908 billion dollars during the last years of the Second World War, and then drops to 109 billion in 1950, the Korean War (1955) immediately brings Pentagon investments back to oscillate around to the 300-400 billion averages, which remained at that level until the new peak of the wars in Afghanistan and the second war in Iraq in the 2000s.

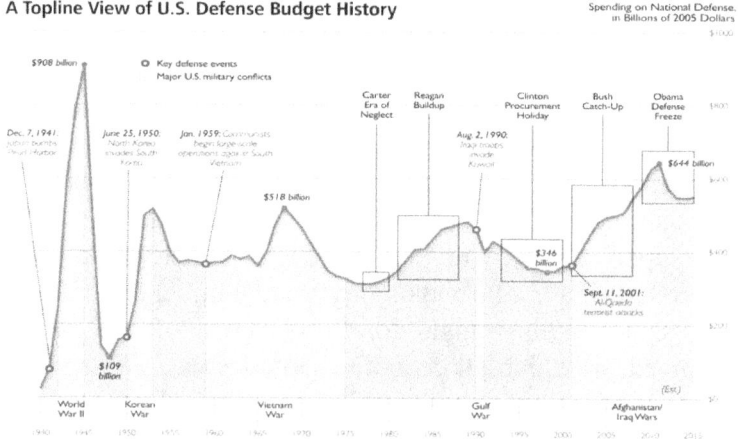

Figure 1 (*previous page*) • The graph represents US defense spending from World War II to today. The peak of the world conflict, never reached again, has contributed to the development of technology in many areas, including computer networks, hardware, and software. Source: Heritage Foundation.

This intense and euphoric activity of reverse engineering (in English: reverse engineering), that is the civil application of products developed for the military sector, will lead not only, thirty years later, to online trading via network technologies, but also to excesses (very "American", after all) such as those told by Philip Corso, lieutenant colonel of the US army, in the book The day after Roswell (The day after Roswell) published in 1997, in which he states that numerous technologies including transistors, lasers, optical fibres, infrared night vision, Kevlar and integrated microcircuits would be derived from the analysis of the remains of an alien flying saucer recovered by the US government in 1947.

In this climate of well-being, cold war, unbridled industrial capitalism closely linked to the needs of the government and expansion of the interests of the United States on a planetary level, comes the aforementioned convergence of finance and telematics, created above all to support the enormous increase in exchanges of stock exchanges registered after the war. An increase that is no longer manageable only by human operators through post, fax or telephone, tools overwhelmed by an incredible amount of paper receipts generated by negotiations now in an explosive growth phase. Suffice it to say that at the beginning of the 1950s in the United States 350,000 shares were traded per year, a number that at the end of the decade became 800,000 units and 2 billion at the end of the 1960s. A research by the

American Stock Exchange carried out in the early 1960s highlights how misregistration of paper orders leads to the United States wasting more than $100 million a year.

A convergence that brings wealth, jobs and an increase in well-being but which, deregulated to excess in the very country in which it developed, will lead to the economic-financial crisis that we are all experiencing right now. Electronic stock exchanges, online derivatives, high-frequency trading, capital trading as an end in itself and without any beneficial impact on the real economy and society, are just some of the elements underlying the current situation. Good tools misused, without real oversight by politics and now partially out of control.

The solution is not, however, to turn off the switch. Rather, it is imagining and concretely applying a new way of using the tools that technology has made available to us. Like? A small example. Between 2001 and 2002 I promoted the creation of operational pages on ethical finance in the weekly "Borsa&Finanza" (of which I have been head of service since 1999). This is not to cheer readers-traders/investors every Saturday, but to indicate a very concrete starting point: that it is possible to earn by investing and trading without further worsening the world around us, giving up a small percentage of the own gain but carefully selecting the companies to which to trust. Because we have now forgotten that trading mostly means trading shares, i.e., parts of companies. And these companies, these banks, these industries that for many are now only tickers, as we have seen in recent months, have a direct impact on society, on people, on the environment, on us. Go to Google and enter the words "corporate social responsibility" (CSR): this will open a new world to which many, for a couple of decades, they are already working without being able to make enough noise.

But before reaching the end of the story, that is to say today, the path will be long and full of events. As anticipated, online trading is based on the convergence of finance with information technology, indeed with its evolution, which is telematics. In other words, these are interconnected computers capable of exchanging data related to capital transactions through more or less regulated markets.

By "computer science" we basically mean computers (hardware), on the one hand, and programs, applications, and languages (software), on the other; with "telematics" all that allows two or more computers to communicate with each other at a distance, either by cable or by radio waves (wireless or wireless). Hardware, networks, finance, and software are therefore the four sectors to follow in order to understand how the current situation has come about. And without the intuitions and ideas of the people who for passion or for work have pushed its evolution beyond the limits of knowledge of each period, it would not have been possible to negotiate shares or derivatives with equipment worthy of the operating rooms of the most sophisticated banks, comfortably at home and sending orders within a few milliseconds.

How positive this is, let us tell the statistics, which indicate that only 20-30% of traders obtain positive results from the activity on the markets and how instead 70-80% constantly lose money. On the other hand, however, the same activity has created thousands of jobs and generated numerous positive effects on the financial markets, including the start of a long phase of unbridled competition that has forced the more conservative banks to redesign their business. around customers rather than just their own interests.

From Sputnik to the Internet

The technology we currently use to trade has evolved, broadly speaking, through numerous leaps that can be schematically summarized as follows:
- before the 1930s: mechanical computers;
- early 1930s -1936: mathematical theoretical basis of automated calculation (Alan Turing, Janos Von Neumann etc.), first processors;
- 1937 1945: first electromechanical analogic and then digital electronic processors;
- 1950 1969: computers isolated from each other (from large mainframes to PCs to minicomputers);
- 1969 1982: interconnected military and university computers (networks, ARPANET);
- 1977 today: computers interconnected by telephone to new and expanding networks (BBS like Fidonet, alternative networks like Usenet, commercial online services like CompuServe);
- 1981 today: terminals interconnected in closed Teletext and Videotex networks (e.g., Minitel);
- 1982 1994: computers interconnected by telephone on an open Internet network;
- 1994 2000: computers interconnected by telephone in an open Internet network through the World Wide Web and browser, convergence of other networks towards the Internet;
- 2000 today: computers and mobile devices interconnected in broadband (ADSL or WiFi);
- in an open network Internet through the World Wide Web and browser.

CHAPTER 1

From the first computers to electronic exchanges

It must be said that computers and networks are composed of dozens and dozens of components that have evolved more or less parallel over time, contributing on different times and ways to the leaps listed above.
Turning moments of this path for online trading were therefore the Second World War for hardware and computing capacity, the 70s with the development of networks, 1994 with the birth of the WWW and finally the 90s. for the development of advanced online trading services as we know them. The recent individual diffusion of broadband is also leading to a new leap forward in software and services. The starting point was the digital computer, or rather, the processor, which bases its existence

on centuries-old studies relating to the ability to perform complex and repetitive calculations with limited human intervention. But without going back to prehistoric times, it is at the beginning of the 1930s that some mathematicians such as Alan Touring, Gottfried Leibniz or Janos Von Neumann laid the theoretical foundations for the development of computational calculation, that is, the way in which it is necessary to provide data to a machine. to process the required result.

However, the fact that only in the early 1940s the first true digital electronic computers were born that is, which do not have mechanical moving parts to perform calculations is no coincidence: the outbreak of the Second World War, as already mentioned, pushes technological research for military purposes to peaks never reached before, concentrating the efforts of the best minds of the time in every field on specific and concrete problems. And the most revolutionary inventions will come out of American and British laboratories and universities, and in some cases even Dutch ones. The result will be terrible tools of destruction but also a legacy of new products, new ideas, new fields of application, new processes and new materials that will change the world forever (or at least until now). After a long series of mechanical and electromechanical computers, in 1936 Alan Touring describes for the first time, but only theoretically, the modern computer model and its components, based on which all future prototypes will be built. The first modern computer ever is considered the ABC, made in 1937, which takes its name from its inventors John Atanasoff and Clifford Berry, hence Atanasoff Berry Computer, precisely ABC. However, the ABC is not yet programmable, a result that Konrad Zuse will reach instead in 1941 with the Z3. Also, in 1937 Koward Aiken, in

collaboration with IBM, creates an electromechanical computer that will have a great impact on the future of the sector, Mark I. The instructions are given to the computer through paper tapes (teleprinter), cards or switches, but its peculiarity is that it is immediately used by the United States Navy. The Mark I is nearly three meters high,
10 meters long, weighs five tons and is cooled with ice. In April 1943 for two months the Red Army rejected Hitler in Stalingrad, reversing the fate of the war, while the US army will soon land in Sicily. In the Pacific, Japan also suffers more than one halt in its initially unstoppable air and naval advance and in those days a bloody battle is underway on the island of Guadalcanal. The Japanese-German resistance, however weakened, is still alive and dangerous. For this reason, the armed forces are frantically searching for tools to shorten the course of the war. One such research focuses on the accuracy of ballistic missiles launched from ships and from the ground. In this climate, John Mauchly and John Eckert of the Moore School of Engineering, Pennsylvania, submit to the authorities the ENIAC a project for a programmable computer capable of calculating complex ballistic trajectories in a few hours. The US Department of Defense does not hesitate to buy the project and carry it out, even if it will not be ready before 1946. It will weigh 30 tons on an area of 180 square meters. Also related to the war is the Colossus, built in the UK by British Telecom's TH Flowers and SW Bradhurst with the collaboration of Alan Touring. The aim is to decrypt Nazi messages encrypted with the famous Enigma machine. Success is full and Colossus could become the backbone of the British computer industry. However, Winston Churchill has it destroyed at the end of the conflict for security reasons.

After the war, the introduction of valves and the new theories on computer programming gave a further boost to the nascent industry, which in 1950 produced what is considered the first minicomputer, the Whirlwind, built at the Massachusetts Institute of Technology in Boston. (MIT). Three years earlier in the Bell laboratories the first transistor came to light, which will be produced starting in 1953, which replaces the large and bulky valves, paving the way for the second generation of electronic computers. From 1948 IBM started the production of electronic calculators for companies, shortly preceded by UNIVAC founded by John Mauchly and John Eckert (those of ENIAC); the latter will sell a total of 46 units of the computer of the same name at a cost of approximately one million dollars each. Its competitor will be the EDSA developed at Cambridge University and marketed by Lyons. These are the years of the development of the first programming languages. One of the first UNIVAC models was purchased by the US government for the population census in 1951, while in 1952 IBM developed the Model 702 for US Defense. Meanwhile in the Netherlands, W. L. Van der Poel of the University of Delft, realizes a computer still based on relays (already replaced by valves).

SAGE, the grandfather of Internet

In 1953 the construction of the most powerful American computer system, the SAGE (SemiAutomatic Ground Environment), was started, developed for the radar protection of the North American territory against possible attacks carried out by Soviet bombers. SAGE (pronounced as the word "wise") will be finished in 1963 and will be used by the Defense until the 1980s. The latter project arises from the geopolitical novelties emerging from the war that are cracking the relations between former allies. The distrust between the Soviet Union and the American and European nations is in fact opening a new phase: the Cold War.

The SAGE, which is one of the most expensive and ambitious military technology projects in US history, is also credited with having greatly contributed to the development of networking technologies. In fact, it is not a single mammoth computer but 23 enormous machines each weighing 113 tons and located in a protected bunker at as many secret offices throughout North America, the latter organized in three separate networks but interconnected by smaller networks, by powerful and redundant computer equipment made mostly by IBM and Burroughs, and by sophisticated management software from Research and Development (RAND).

The latter, which, as we will see, will have a leading role in the development of the network that will become the Internet, in 1955 created the non-profit company System Development Corporation (SDC) and made it available to the US Defense precisely for the SAGE project. The connections between the 23 offices take place through normal telephone networks (supplied by Bell System) connected by modems, devices capable of "modulating-demodulating" the digital signals received, that is, of interpreting them.

The SAGE computers, the AN I FQ7s, designed by MIT Lincoln Laboratory and built by IBM (which will raise about $500 million from the operation), are hidden deep underground; they receive data from a hundred microwave radars invented by physicist George Valley scattered over the continent, process them, and enable semi-automated military responses, being connected with missile systems that can be activated remotely by human operators.

Due to its enormous cost (estimated at between 8 and 12 billion dollars at the time), to its very wide technological, social and production implications, and to the great research and development effort initiated in all directions by the companies involved, SAGE is considered the real starting point of the US and world IT industry, through which the founders of the largest hi-tech groups in the USA that will develop in the following decades will pass as contractors, subcontractors and consultants.

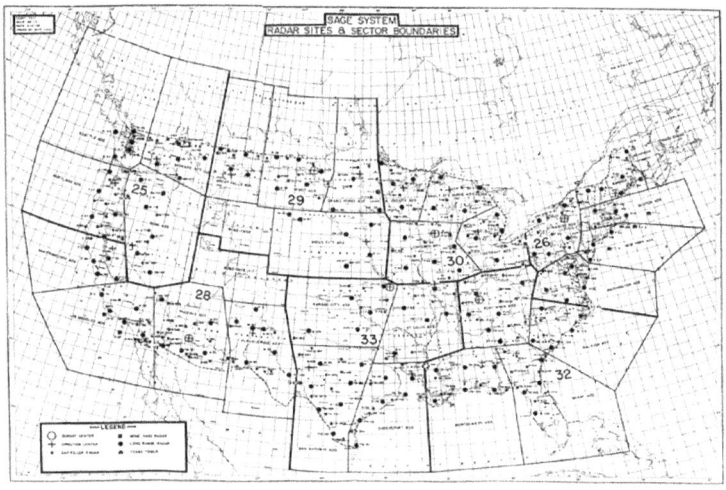

Figure 2 • The map of the SAGE (Semi-Automatic Ground Environment), a telematic system of interconnected radar developed by the US Defense from 1953 to 1963 for the interception of Soviet bombers. The technology developed for this project will be the basis of the Arpanet first and then of the Internet

In these years, therefore, the first true geographic computer network was created, a sign that this side of technology has also developed considerably. But how?

Everything comes from the first great electromechanical computers. Initially, in fact, they are not programmable, so it is necessary to provide them with the information by opening and closing switches (then valves and transistors) when the necessary procedure for the calculation itself is needed. To simplify the process, systems are developed to supply previously prepared data to machines that are now equipped with memory: fax machines and punch card reading systems are connected to the computer which make the large machine "swallow" kilometers of paper or magnetic tapes. Later, video terminals will be connected to the computers for managing the data entered: the bridge thus created between the central body of the computer and the terminal constitutes the core of the first computer network.

Each company will then develop, over the decades, its own devices, specifications, and protocols for the transmission of data via cable and it will have to wait until 1977 for the foundation of OSI, an international organization for the standardization of computer networks and its hardware components. and software. The best known and most widely used of these protocols is TCP I IP, now used for data transmissions via the Internet and developed since the 1980s based on a long series of predecessors. And right at the heart of the Internet is SAGE.

As anticipated, in fact, it was the Cold War that gave a new impetus to investments in technology. The shot forward took place on October 4, 1957, when the Soviet Union amazed the world and sent the first satellite, Sputnik, into orbit, proving that at that moment it had a technology superior to that of the United States.

The race for space, but also for rearmament, has begun. To react to the inferiority situation, the following year the US Department of Defense creates the Advanced Research Projects Agency (ARPA), which takes on the long-term development of military technologies; only later will NASA be assigned the management of space programs.

Figure 3 • The reaction of the US newspapers in the aftermath of the announcement of the launch of Sputnik, which took place on 4 October 1957

Figure 4 • The cover of "Life" of November 18, 1957, which compares the space projects of the United States and the Soviet Union

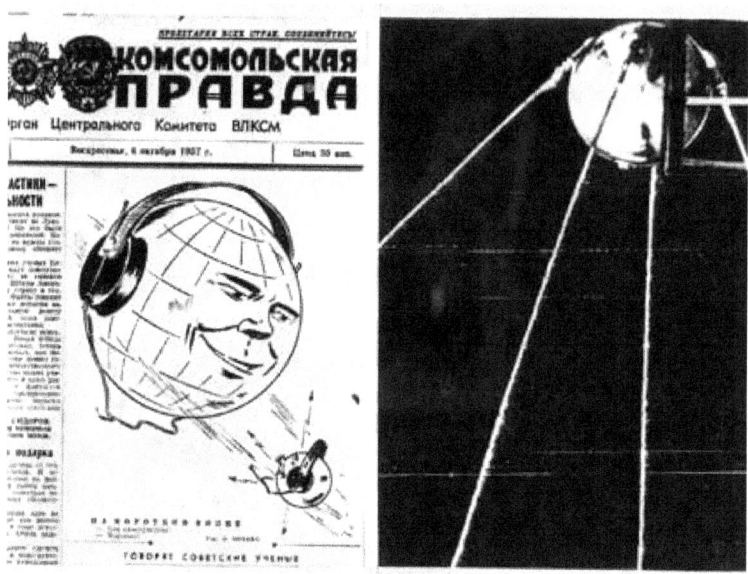

Figure 5 • The first page of the Russian newspaper "Pravda", which celebrates the launch of Sputnik two days after the event

ARPAnet

Still active, the ARPA (whose name will be changed to DARPA several times over the decades, adding and removing the initial of Defense) starting from 1962 constitutes a division in charge of developing the network technologies created for the SAGE and of apply them not only to air defense but also to the army and navy. In the summer of the same year Paul Baran, engineer of RAND (as we have already seen active in the SAGE project) and previously employed at Hughes Aircraft (the group founded by Howard Hughes: who does not remember "The Aviator", the film by Martin Scorsese with Leonardo Di Caprio who plays the great and eccentric industrialist?), presents to the first director of the division, Joseph Licklider, a "packet switching" data transmission project developed in the course of research for SAGE, with which a digitized message is sent in the form of many packets and scattered through a computer network which in turn are able to route the received packets to their final destination, putting in order and thus reconstructing the original message.

A very suitable system for connecting a network of military installations: if, in fact, one was put out of use by a bombing, the message would not be interrupted as it would happen using a normal telephone line but would still be able to reach the receiver. It is the first step towards what will be the TCP I IP protocol which is the basis of the Arpanet network and then of the Internet.

A few months earlier, exactly on May 31, 1961, an obscure researcher from the Massachusetts Institute of Technology in Boston (USA), Leonard Kleinrock, based on the ideas of the Polish-American scientist Paul Baran, published an article on the theoretical possibility of carrying out data transmissions via packet-switched cable. The article will become his doctoral thesis at the University of California Los Angeles (UCLA), which will lead Kleinrock, on October 29, 1969, to make for the first time in the world a connection between two computers, one located at his own University, the other at the Stanford Research Institute. The ARPANET network initially includes only military centers, universities and IT companies involved in advanced research coordinated by the Defense. With the creation of specific networks for military and university use only, the developed protocols and technologies will be privatized, and service providers will multiply since the 1990s and, for a fee, will offer companies and individuals the connection to the Internet, which takes place via modem. on normal telephone lines (dial-up).

Parallel to and outside the Internet, in 1977, numerous proprietary networks and the bulletin board system (bulletin board system) developed; the latter allow multiple users to connect to a central computer at the same time and use it as a means of exchanging files, messages and communications. From the mid-1990s, proprietary networks and BBSs will gradually converge on the Internet.

Compared to the United States, up to the 1970s the rest of the world was therefore technologically a step behind, even when it comes to countries that invested considerable resources in the sector. Among these, the Soviet Union and Japan are at the forefront, closely followed by the United Kingdom, which enjoys the transfer of ideas and resources from the USA and the permanent presence of the large American IT groups, and from France.

In addition to ARPANET, however, starting from 1968 in the USA other telephone networks developed at the same time, used specifically for the connection between computers, defined WANs, i.e., World Area Networks, including, for example, Tymnet, Telenet and Uninet.

The first, built on its own by a time-sharing company founded in 1964 and founded by Norm Hardy and LaRoy Tymes, was closed in 2004 after being sold over the years to McDonnell Douglas, British Telecom, MCI Worldcom, AT&T and finally to Verizon. Telenet (not to be confused with the Telnet network protocol) became operational on August 16, 1975, based on the experience of the founders (Leo Beranek and Richard Bolt, MIT professors, and Robert Newman, one of their students) as contractors for the military network ArpaNet; their work will make a significant contribution to the development of electronic mail, network protocols, some programming languages and more. Telenet was then taken over by Sprint who renamed it Sprintnet and then Sprintlink, when it merged with the Internet which has now become public.

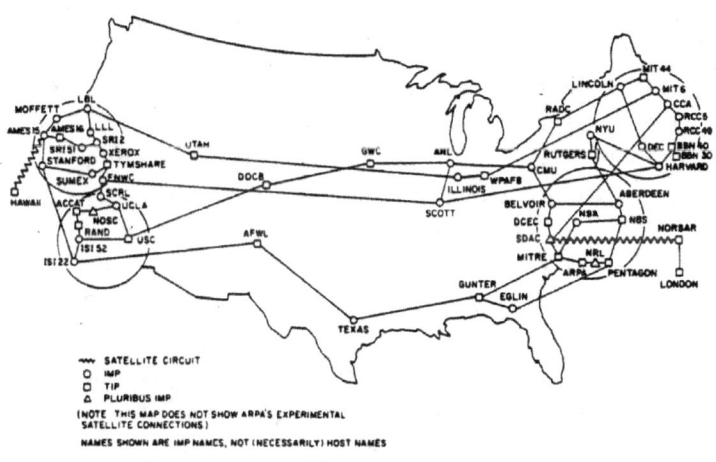

Figure 6 • The Arpanet network in July 1977

USSR and Japan

In the USSR, the production of computers, based on the pioneering work of Sergei Lebedev and Isaak Bruk, is strictly reserved for the military and university fields, but starting from 1979 the detachment of the West becomes unbridgeable: in that year the Soviet Union invades Afghanistan and the USA, in reaction, prohibit the export of information technology to the great rival, not to mention that the absence of an internal private market stifles any autonomous development.

In Japan, however, things are different. Here, it is not the Defense that is pushing the accelerator of information technology, but it is the large companies first and, subsequently, the Ministry of Commerce and Industry. The first all-Japanese computer, the Fujic, made by Okazaki Bunkji of Fuji, dates to 1956. The real father of Japanese computer science, however, is Muroga Saburo, who improves many technical aspects of Western discoveries especially in the direction of better efficiency and miniaturization, for example by adopting transistors ahead of their time. The creation of large consortia between IT manufacturers (e.g., between NEC, Hitachi, and Fujitsu) gives rise to an almost unknown phenomenon in the USA: the standardization of components, designed to be used freely on products of consortium companies.

After an initial Japanese boom, in the 1990s, however, the decline of the local industry followed due to the strong expansion of US companies, due to the ability to offer highly localized products. Subsequently, the resumption of the "Asian tigers" brought this region of the world back to the top in research and development, so much so that in the 2000s there were only three large, printed circuit factories and all three were in Taiwan, built with Japanese capital.

The automation of finance: ECN, telematic exchanges and SWIFT

In the 1960s, therefore, the bulk of the discoveries and their applications to corporate computing products were made. And in the meantime, how has finance evolved?
First, it is necessary to distinguish two successive stages of development of electronic transactions: the "internal" and the "external" to banks. The first concerns the management of processes and cash flows, the securities portfolio, treasury, administration, logistics and more, functions that the bank, as a company, performs to optimize its business. This category also includes transactions and exchanges of information and data with other banks and with institutions, including the so-called clearing and settlement, i.e., the offsetting of interbank flows and exchanges. The second level concerns the connection with customers and the services offered to them.
Obviously, before offering telematic services to individuals and companies, banks and financial intermediaries began to use telematics technology for themselves, to find new ways, that is, to reduce costs, increase speed, be more competitive and beat the competition. Opening a direct connection to their mainframes for customers was the next step.
The first attempts date back to the 1950s: from 1959 the "Magnetic Ink Character Recognition" (MICR), machines

for automated check reading, spread in banks, then between 1960 and 1970 they were developed and spread in Europe, in the United States and then in the rest of the world the Automated Teller Machines (ATM, which in Italy will be called Bancomat) for the withdrawal of cash.

British Barclays installed the first in 1967 at the Enfield branch in London. At the end of 1985 there will be 50,000 throughout the United States, 40,000 in Japan and 25,000 in Europe, mostly in France (1,600 from Crédit Agricole alone) and Belgium. Both MICR and ATM are connected to electronic networks that speed up repetitive operations.

An important starting point for the development of banking telematic activities can be found once again in the 1950s, in England. Here in 1955 Barclays placed itself at the head of the Committee of London Clearing Bankers (CLCB) an interbank committee charged with "promoting discussion and research on developments in the field of mechanization with particular reference to electronic ones and their applicability to banking practices and impact of these developments on personnel problems".

The Sub-Committee starts a series of talks with the main British and US computer manufacturers to develop common standards and in 1959, after installing an Emidec 1100 transistor processor made by the British EMI Electronics (costing £ 125,000), Barclays becomes the first English bank to send an order via computer. In 1961, Barclays inaugurated the first banking computer center in the United Kingdom. But Barclays is proceeding practically in parallel with numerous other banks, preceded in the use of computers and in the mechanization of branches by only a few months. Thus, Martins Bank installs a Ferranti Pegasus II in September 1961, followed by Coutts Bank (with a Univac SS 80 STEP), Lloyds (with three IBM RAMACs),

Midland Bank (English Electric KDP 10), National Provincial Bank (Ferranti Orion), Westminster Bank (IBM 1401), Bank of Scotland (IBM 1401) and many others. However, Bank of Scotland had already installed an IBM 402 tabulator, the predecessor of computers, in its Edinburgh office in 1959.

Across the Atlantic, meanwhile, the Stanford Research Institute presented in September 1955 the Electronic Recording Method of Accounting (ERMA), a computerized system for processing banking activities developed at the request of Bank of America, which will be built by General Electric and installed starting in the fall of 1956. Bank of America alone will install 32.

As we can see, the IT ferment in the banking sector (and the British one is just one example) began in the early years of the Cold War. The real first step in the direction of online financial transactions, however, came in 1961, when the US Congress authorized the Securities and Exchange Commission (SEC) to conduct a study on the excessive fragmentation of the so-called over-the-counter (OTC) market, trading in financial securities that take place outside regulated markets. Many operators, in fact, meet outside the stock exchanges and physically exchange the securities of listed companies. It takes some time, but in 1963 the SEC released the results of the research, concluding that to reduce the phenomenon capable of altering the peaceful trend of the markets it is necessary to focus on the automation of processes. The next step is therefore to pass the ball to the National Association of Securities Dealers (NASD), an association founded in 1934 which over time has become by law the self-regulated body to which all authorized financial intermediation companies in the USA must register; broadly speaking, it can be said that in the Anglo-Saxon world, dealers are intermediaries whose profit is represented by the difference between the purchase price and the sale price (bid-ask spread), while brokers are those who are remunerated through a commission received from clients.

It will take eight years, but the results, as we shall see, will amaze the world of capital. In the meantime, the legislation allows the birth of a new type of securities trading circuit, the ECN (Electronic Communication Network), i.e., an automated system with its own rules but still subject to the control of state supervision, through which financial intermediaries can trade securities with each other outside regulated markets. Over time, ECNs will be able to connect directly to the same exchanges, now online, and integrate with them (and in many cases end up being acquired by the exchanges themselves). The first electronic trading circuit in history saw the light on June 25, 1968, when Alan Kay, an IT expert, created a management system for the automated exchange that he called AutEx, from Automatic Exchange. After having unsuccessfully proposed it to the NYSE, Kay launched the electronic stock exchange project by himself, founding the company AutEx Service Corporation in Boston and officially presenting the project at the New York Chamber of Commerce in the presence of 180 representatives of US financial companies. The first intermediaries registered to AutEx as members are Wellington, Massachusetts Investors Trust, Putnam, and Fidelity. AutEx allows you to view the proposals on your computer, organized in small, medium, and large blocks or with indicated limits and the name of the bidder, but for negotiation, contact must in any case be made by telephone. The system uses Sigma computers produced by Scientific Data System (SDS) and requires institutional investors $200 a month, which for brokers instead becomes $5,000. AutEx continued the business for ten years, then in 1978 its founder sold the company to Thomson Financial (later Thomson Reuters), which still today offers the Thomson Reuters Autex Block Data and the Thomson Reuters Autex Trade Route among its services. Over the years Alan Kay has revealed himself to be an eccentric idealist as well as a farsighted and visionary entrepreneur. Kay founded in 1954 the research company for military purposes TRG; he has in fact written numerous books against the war and for the reform of society, the State and the Internet, coming to propose a complete restructuring of the Internet on totally new bases, renaming it Betternet, for eliminate the risks associated with the presence of those he defines as "pranksters, sociopaths, terrorists, hackers and virus spreaders", but also to restore efficiency, especially as regards peer-to-peer connections, that is, directly between users. He wrote an autobiography with a significant title: "Militarist, millionaire, peacenik".

On his website (http://www.alanfkay.com) you can view his theories. In 1969, the New York company Institutional Networks, founded by Jerome Pustilnik and Herbert Behrens, was born from technological foundations developed by companies with close ties to military circles: the new ECN in 1985 will take the abbreviated name of Instinet and is still today active. It is still a service only for institutional investors (in 1971 it will register the participation of about 30 banks and financial companies), but it is an important first step. Ultimately, the era of telematic finance begins with Instinet.

Shortly before, in 1964, Bunker Ramo, a company specializing in military electronic equipment, now integrated into Honeywell, was born in Trumbull, Connecticut (United States). The two founders are George Bunker and Simon Ramo. To get an idea of who we are talking about, Ramo is a physicist known as the father of ICBMs and the application of microwaves. In the 1940s he worked for the aerospace group founded by Howard Hughes (such as the a forementioned Paul Baran, one of the inventors of packet switching) developing advanced radar systems and missile systems in close contact with the United States Defense, to then collaborate with NASA to develop launch vectors for satellites. His partner George Bunker is instead a senior executive of the military industrial group Martin Marietta, with which the Bunker Ramo was founded in a joint venture.

In 1968 NASD commissioned Bunker Ramo to develop an innovative electronic trading system. Shortly thereafter, the competitor New York Stock Exchange (NYSE) also announced the project to create a system which, however, will retain the presence of specialists, the Block Automated System (BAS). On February 8, 1971, it was Bunker Ramo that unveiled to the world the revolutionary telematic trading system for financial securities created by its Information Systems Division on behalf of the NASD. The system is called NASDAQ, adding to the acronym of the association two final letters that simply indicate "Automated Quotations", thus obtaining an acronym that means "Automated Quotes of the NASD": it is the outcome of the assignment entrusted by the SEC to the NASD in 1963. Even today, on the NASDAQ website, it is possible to view a historical video showing the headquarters of the Bunker Ramo in which the enormous IT infrastructures necessary to make the newborn digital market work have just been installed. The NASDAQ system was created to allow NASD associates to exchange, in a safe and fast environment, over-the-counter (OTC) securities, i.e., not yet listed on one of the then existing stock exchanges (including New York Stock Exchange or NYSE, active since at least 1817); only from 1975 will it become a real stock exchange by acquiring the regulated market license to list only shares placed on its own market and separating the OTC securities from the main trades.

The 1975 qualitative leap is allowed by a series of amendments to the Securities Exchange Act by which the United States Government creates the National Securities Market (NSM), starting a process of liberalization and incentives to the financial sector that by 1987 it will lead to a tenfold increase in stock market volumes. A decision that, ironically, arises from the request by the NYSE to increase the registration fees that the law obliged dealers to pay when they wanted to join the stock exchange. The intervention of the Department of Justice, aimed at blocking the perpetuation of the monopolistic practice that blocks the development of the sector, led the US Congress, precisely in 1975, to remove this taxing power from the NYSE. The move gives life in a few months to a new category of intermediaries, the discount brokers, who can lower brokerage commissions to make their services also accessible to individuals.

Competition in the financial intermediation sector takes off

In 1976 NASD took over all the tools and infrastructures developed for trading from the Bunker Ramo, thus starting to manage the processes internally. This change will allow

NASDAQ (which has been a separate company from NASD since 2006) to compete directly with the NYSE in terms of traded volumes and listed companies (but not in terms of overall capitalization), also thanks to a series of mergers. and acquisitions, including those featuring the American Stock Exchange, the Philadelphia Stock Exchange, and the Scandinavian group of stock exchanges OMX.

After NASDAQ, the second exchange to implement a fully electronic trading service in 1980 is the Cincinnati Stock Exchange, which will later become the National Stock Exchange (NSX). Two years after the inauguration of the NASDAQ, a much more ambitious project will come to life, the SWIFT. It is an interbank electronic payment system managed by the Society for Worldwide Interbank Financial Telecommunication based in Brussels which, at its start in 1977 in the presence of the then Prince (now King) Albert of Belgium, involves 239 banks from 15 countries in Worldwide. Forty years later, as of September 2011, it boasts 10,005 members (including 2,326 banks and numerous central banks) in 209 countries, with a number of interbank contacts in excess of 3.3 billion. A huge, predominantly European network that silently extends its tentacles across the globe year after year.

SWIFT, whose development began in 1973, is perhaps the most widespread platform for financial transactions for professional use in the world and is based on codified standards, collectively defined as FEDI (Financial Electronic Data Interchange, i.e., "financial interchange of electronic data"). whose drafting began in the 1960s.

According to international definitions, Financial EDIs are exchanges of electronic data equivalent to the exchange of documents: this means that banks and financial institutions around the world have been exchanging data, contracts, orders for transfers of funds and electronic documents for forty years, all with binding legal value, through coded electronic systems accepted by all, thus saving billions of tons of paper, and reducing the impact of errors on financial processes. The FIX (Financial Information Exchange) circuit also works on this basis, through which stock exchange data and information regarding listed securities from all over the world flow. It is a transmission protocol developed since 1992.

Among the first attempts to regulate the transfer of funds by technological means is the Electronic Funds Transfer Act, signed in 1978 by the US president Jimmy Carter, which establishes the rights of users in terms of information, identification, receipt of paper documents. if required, insurance in the event of theft or system failure, and so on.

Finally, in 1982, the US Congress passed the Tax Equity and Fiscal Responsibility Act (TEFRA), a law that modifies the tax legislation for banks and which among other things obliges financial intermediaries to provide copious amounts of information to federal agencies. Obligation that intermediaries can only fulfill by equipping themselves with an IT structure capable of collecting and processing data very quickly.

The TEFRA, therefore, like other similar laws in other countries, represents one of the incentives that forcefully push finance towards telematics. This excursus on bank payment systems, deliberately brief and more than concise, is only an indication of a phenomenon that cannot be overlooked considering the history of telematic finance: banks and financial companies began to develop systems very early on. of electronic transactions, but they did it for themselves, that is, to satisfy their own internal needs, not at all related to the needs of customers. Or at least, having this as the last of my thoughts.

The telematization of data exchange processes between different companies and then internal to the various branches of the companies themselves (divisions, branches, etc.) subsequently spread to all levels, finally reaching, with corporate banking, home banking and then with online trading, even to customers. A phenomenon that will be repeated even later precisely in online trading, with the spread to retail of professional services, functions and platforms used within the operating rooms of financial institutions.

However, only through pharaonic projects, very expensive but strongly focused, such as SAGE, ARPAnet or SWIFT, has it been possible to grant the "mass" some technological crumbs. But in some countries more than others, where individual initiative is promoted, sustained and an integral part of socio-economic growth, these crumbs have been taken and transformed into entire bakeries. Beyond metaphor, in the United States, Germany and Great Britain especially the fallout from these major projects over the decades have transformed industry, communications, education, information, politics and, ultimately, the whole society.

The birth of home banking: Videotex and tone phones

In the wake of liberalization, at the end of the 1980s the first services for sending orders for the trading of financial securities appeared in the United States through tone-tone telephone keypads intended for private users. The digitization of exchanges and ECNs has in fact reduced costs and simplified procedures, but computers are not yet widespread enough among private individuals to be able to create mass trading services at sufficiently low costs.

The telephone, on the other hand, is a tool that is present in all homes and offices and is cheap. It is no coincidence, as we shall see, that similar services will be developed in Europe at the same time (starting from Germany and the United Kingdom).

Similarly, in the 1970s a series of services were born in the Old Continent, specifically in the United Kingdom, which go under the name of Videotex and which in the individual countries will be baptized in different ways (in France Minitel, in Italy Videotel etc.). These are closed and centralized networks, mostly managed by telecommunications monopolists, based on the X25 protocol but not integrated with each other. Marketed with small terminals equipped with basic graphics and keyboards, they are connected to the normal telephone network and offer information services (telephone directories, train, and airplane timetables, etc.) and the purchase of agreed goods and services.

Although offered for a long time, Videotex will have little success mainly due to the high time connection costs, while in the United States they will only have an impromptu diffusion. Of all these, today only the French Minitel can boast a widespread diffusion and be considered a commercial success; it is still active, although it is expected to close in 2012.

Since this is a service now killed by the Internet, it could be almost useless to talk about it, if not as a historical curiosity.

However, Teletext and Videotex services represented the first real online channel in the banking sector, which for at least a decade has tried to grow and develop. A channel that did not live up to expectations not so much because of the network technology that supported it, but more because of the negative perception of the relationship between cost and benefit by end users. The costs, in other words, of the terminal, of the service and of the connection were always kept too high by the suppliers (and we will see why) and this compromised any possibility of widespread diffusion.

First of all it is good to distinguish between Teletext and Videotex: the first is a service created by television channel managers to send simple information over the air to home televisions and is therefore unidirectional (the user only receives and views information), as in the case of the still existing homonymous service provided by the Italian RAI; the second is instead developed by telecommunications companies that manage telephone networks, on which it is possible to carry out bidirectional transmissions (the user receives information and makes choices by re-sending information in turn) through precisely small terminals specially made, as is this was the case of the Videotel of SIP and as it is still that of the French Minitel.

Both technologies are developed in the United Kingdom between the 1960s and 1970s, and both have a "defect of origin" that weakens their growth potential: they are produced by monopolists or large state-owned companies. free from internal competition. This feature, if on the one hand it will make it lucky in the first years of launch within the countries in which the individual monopolists are based for the possibility of mobilizing huge human and financial resources, of using large scientific laboratories, of rapidly penetrating and capillary market, all thanks to the support of the State will push to keep the price too high for the end user, even limiting its adoption in other countries, and will prevent the creation of a single standard capable of making all systems interoperable and thus create a large European network of telematic services. Nationalistic jealousies but also the strong initial investments for development will in fact curb the further financial effort required for the convergence of the various systems.

The two initial protagonists of Teletext and Videotex are General Post Office (GPO), a British monopolist of the postal and telecommunications service (which will later be divided into Post Office and British Telecom), and British Broadcasting Corporation, i.e., the state-run radio and television company BBC, affectionately called Beeb by the British. In 1968 (the year in which, as mentioned, Alan Kay presented the first telematic exchange, AutEx in the United States), the engineer Geoff Larkby and the technician Barry Pyatt of the Designs Department (Television Group) of the BBC, production of subtitles for television broadcasts, are commissioned by the general manager Hugh Carleton Green to create a text transmission system that allows users to send "the equivalent of a page from the Times" to their home televisions and to be able to print it comfortably at home, with particular attention to the prices of raw materials and publicly traded equities.

Testing the result of the first service, called Beebfax, fails and the experiment is suspended, while the two leave the BBC: Larkby retires, Pyatt changes company. A few months later, however, the project was resumed on the basis of what the two former employees had done, and the Ceefax Teletext service was born, in which name is a pun based on BB-C fax, more or less "the printable service of Beeb".

Announced in 1972 and became operational on September 23, 1974, it is expected to be suspended in April 2012.

```
CEEFAX 1  100  Sun     5 Oct   23:56
BBC CEEFAX
East Sport
ALL THE LATEST SPORT FROM YOUR AREA 390

A-Z INDEX            199  NEWS HEADLINES      101
BBC INFO             695  NEWS FOR REGION     160
CHESS                568  NEWSROUND           570
COMMUNITY BBC2       650  RADIO        BBC1   640
ENTERTAINMENT        500  READ HEAR    BBC2   640

FILM REVIEWS         526  SPORT               300
FINANCE     BBC2     200  SUBTITLING          888
FLIGHTS              440  TOP 40              528
GAMES REVIEWS        527  TRAVEL              430
HORSERACING          660  TV LINKS            615
LOTTERY              555  TV LISTINGS         600
SCI-TECH             154  WEATHER             400

     Ceefax: The world at your fingertips
```

Figure 7 A screenshot of the Ceefax service, provided by the BBC through the normal home television. Note the item "Finance"

Shortly thereafter, the British communications authority, the IBA, promoted a competing system developed by the ITV television channel in 1974 and called Oracle; in 1976, however, the systems will be made intercompatible and merged into what will be called World System Teletext, which will then be sold to televisions in many European countries and the United States.

Almost simultaneously, GPO launched a first two-way Videotex service with Viewdata technology, invented in

1968 by Samuel Fedida, engineer, and computer applications manager at the British Post Office Research Laboratories. The first commercial prototype will be ready in 1974, tested on HP minicomputers, and will be launched in early 1979. Viewdata technology is based on the V.23 transmission protocol (1,200 bits per second in reception and 75 in transmission) and the service was initially created as a channel for travel agencies, which can thus provide customers with information on dates, departures, or availability to organize and book holidays. The name under which Viewdata will be marketed in the UK is Prestel. The development of the English market (which will in any case be limited to no more than 90,000 users at the time of maximum expansion) gives way to the development of other systems by the national "champions" of local telecommunications.

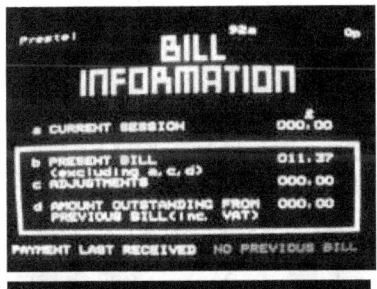

Figure 8 • Some images of Prestel, the English Videotext service (1980)

Thus, in France, in 1972 the CCETT (National Research Center for Television and Telecommunications) started the development of Antiope, a Teletext slower than the Prestel (data compression is 30% lower) but more sophisticated. However, it will have a short life: the 9 million European users of Prestel will prevail over the 100,000 of Antiope, which will be closed in 1987. But it is precisely from the experience that Antiope will be launched in 1982 by PTT (Poste, Téléphone et Télécommunications, in 1991 broken into two sections France Télécom and La Poste) the Videotex called Minitel and invented by the engineer Jean-Yves Pouchard. In 1977 two researchers, Alain Minc and Simon Nora, presented to the President of the Republic Valéry Giscard d'Estaing a report on the state of computerization of French society, signaling an imminent telematic revolution based on access to information via terminals.

In fact, in a few years in Canada, Japan, France and the United Kingdom similar services for the transmission of simple texts and images have been developed and the computerization of the Hexagone (nickname that the French give to their country) should be based on this.

Taking up the suggestion, in 1978 the Ministry of Posts and Communications of Paris then launched the project of a public Videotex service and in 1982 the PPT launched, with strong state subsidies, a service with innovative characteristics: the terminal, developed by Alcatel, it is given free of charge to all telephone subscribers and allows you to connect via telephone cable to a large number of services, from air and train ticketing, to searching for telephone numbers, from searching for information to databases to financial services. The connection takes place not through the Internet's TCP I IP protocol but with the Transpac X25, which is not very suitable for high-speed data transmission.

It will be one of the greatest European technological successes, reaching one million units installed in 1985, which became nine million in 1999 for an estimated 25 million users.

Canada and Japan, as mentioned, have already joined the fray, the first with the Videotex system called Telidon (1978), the second, developed by the telecommunications giant NTT, with Captain (1979-80), to which the West Germany with the Bildschirmtext (or BTX, developed from 1976 by IBM for Deutsche Bundespost and launched in 1983, based on a mix of features of the Minitel and the Postel) and then Sweden with a Prestel integrated with additional features.

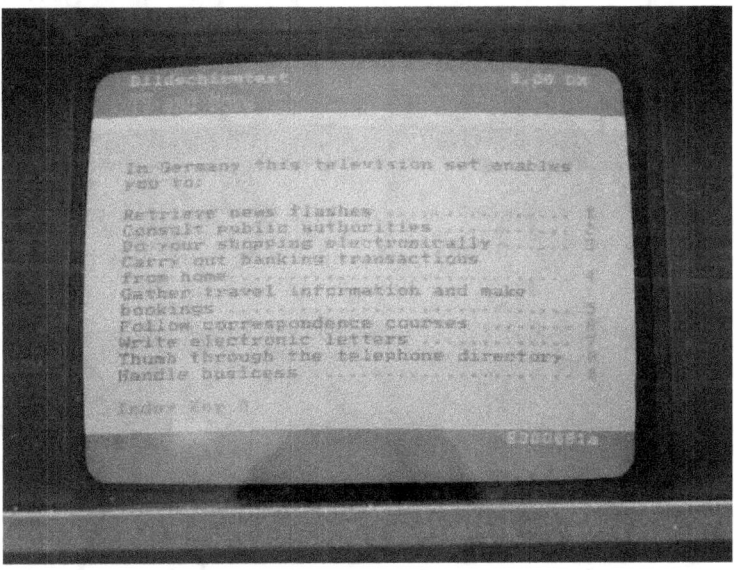

Figure 9 • An image dating back to 1987 from the German Videotex, called Bildschirmtext or BTX. On the fourth line of the menu, the indication "Carry out banking transactions from home" can be read

As early as 1978, countries will try to standardize their respective systems, but the numerous international technical conferences reveal only the unwillingness of the participants: the investments were too large and the commercial results too poor to invest in convergence and thus see an increase in competition. For this, four different standards are created (CEPT 1, 2, 3 and 4) with the mild recommendation (which will never be implemented) that, in the event of a future update, the individual systems aim for convergence.

What happens instead is that the struggle is unleashed between the competing French and British systems to occupy the largest number of foreign markets with their own standard, starting with the United States.

Here only AT&T enters the market in 1981 with a system derived from the Canadian Telidon, which in 1983 will be called NAPLPS. In Videotex-risiko, English Prestel is adopted by telecommunications or service companies in Australia, Austria, Belgium, Germany, Italy (180,000 users), Yugoslavia, Hong Kong, New Zealand, the Netherlands, Singapore, Hungary and other Countries, while the Minitel in turn sells the service in French-speaking countries as well as in China and Brazil.

Figure 10 • The Brazilian Videotexto in 1982, based on the English Prestel. Again, some financial services are available

Figure 11 • The Brazilian Videotexto in 1982: the second item of the initial menu indicates "Banks, stock exchanges, economy and finance"

But the United States is the real battleground of the two different systems. A clamorous example of this is the report made by the magazine "New Scientist" on November 27, 1980, in the article entitled "French and British slug it out in teletext battle". The story arises from the request by the British Ministry of Industry to the US government to make the English system the standard in the US by law, in this supporting a request made by the IBA (English Independent Broadcasting Authority) and by a large patrol of British industrial groups involved in the project and holders of the patents of what is recognized as "the Britain's six-years-old invention". Technically, all televisions need to change the radio signals they send to home televisions.

To unravel the tangle of domestic and international pressures, in a deal worth billions of dollars, the Federal Communications Commission (FCC) creates a committee that brings together the most interested US companies and asks them to choose between the English, French and Canadian. A week before the verdict, CBS contacts the FCC and presses for Antiope to be chosen. In the end, the British get more votes than the French, but no one reaches the quorum of 75% of the required votes and the FCC will advise Washington not to set any standard, but to let the market do it: that companies are free to choose the standard they prefer, the competition will help the growth of the sector, cut costs and give oxygen to more efficient services. The comment of the "New Scientist" is that "in reality, the two services are practically identical, differing only in the cost of the terminals". However, the anonymous columnist breaks a lance in favour of Antiope, "closer to the American systems" (derived from the Canadian ones, in whose development France has not by chance played a secondary role) also because Informatique, the company that markets the French system in the US, "has already provided The Source with 250,000 low-cost terminals for its information services", each of which costs the user $600, "and has also signed an agreement with Tymnet".

On European and North American soil, therefore, there is a fight for the future of banking and financial services via Videotex, the first true technology for corporate and home banking.

Above all on these bases, but not only, the first generation of rudimentary online trading services will develop within a few years, provided, as we will see, through online services such as CompuServe, Prodigy, America On Line, The Source and others. Ten years before the World Wide Web was born.

From a security point of view, however, Videotex still has a long way to go. In 1984, for example, two hackers sneak into the Duke of Edinburgh's private mailbox on the Prestel. The scandal, known in the press of the time as "the royal connection", not only deeply damaged Prestel's reputation, but showed that there are still no legal instruments to prosecute the guilty; in 1988 "Mr. Gold and Mr. Schifreen" (as the two hackers are called in the legal documents concerning them) are acquitted of the charge of "forgery "(forgery of passwords) and the judge dryly comments that" their conduct was essentially that of having accessed Prestel relevant data with a trick. This is not a crime. If it were deemed desirable that it was, this is a matter for the Legislator rather than the Court. However, during the trial it is specified that the violated box of the Duke is not the private one but only a demonstrative one, while Gold and Schifreen define its content as "boring" and mostly linked to the birth of the Duke's son. Two years later the British Parliament promulgates the "Computer Misuse Act". The

German BTX is the victim of a perhaps even more sensational case, again in 1984: a technoanarchist group from Hamburg known as CCC, which uses BTX to offer some online services, manages to obtain the password of the central computer of a bank. local, Hamburg Sparkasse, instructing them to continually contact their paid service via BTX. The bank thus unknowingly accumulates a debt of approximately 135,000 marks towards the CCC. The latter, however, reveals the scam to the press, refusing the payment but also in this case seriously damaging the growth ambitions of the German Videotex. From the early 1980s, the development of European online finance will take place parallel to that of the United States. According to former Chevy Chase Bank vice president, Robert Spicer (quoted in a 1997 book by Mary Cronin), home banking has been studied by banks since the mid-1970s to reduce back-office costs. particularly those deriving from automated services carried out with touch-tone phones (touch-tone phones, as we will see later). The first known example of home banking in the United States is the Channel 2000 service created in 1980 by Banc One (which became Bank One in 2004 after the acquisition by JP Morgan).

At the launch, CEO John McCoy said when he asked the board of directors to increase the R&D budget, the members replied, "We are a bank, what should we look for?". And despite the technological novelty that McCoy can show off shortly thereafter, his board is perhaps not entirely wrong to be sceptical: Channel 2000 collects only 200 customers and is quickly replaced by a new version of the service, Applause. However, this too does not exceed 1,000 users and is abandoned: according to the bank's calculations, home banking must reach at least 5,000 customers to support itself with its own legs.

Figure 12 • An advertisement for Bank One's home banking service

Channel 2000 we read in the official story of Banc One/Bank One drawn up in 2008 by the parent company JP Morgan Chase "allowed the bank's customers to see the balances of their transactions on the television screen, as well as to pay bills and make transfers", all "operating on normal telephone lines". The same story, however, describes Channel 2000 as "one of the first online home banking services": a sign that there were probably others already active that have been lost, confirming the words of Robert Spicer.

Another indication of the presence of several banks interested in the development of remote services for private customers is the fact that from the "New York Times" of March 1983 we learn that Banc One itself gives life to Videofinancial Services, a joint venture with Southeast Banking, Wachovia and Security Pacific to offer other institutions a Covidea-branded home banking service through Viewtron, the Videotex system developed by AT&T with Knight-Ridder Newspapers on the NAPLPS protocol. In October 1983, in turn, the US telecommunications giant and the Florida publisher, through the subsidiary Viewdata, will start marketing a service for online purchases ("computerized shopping", as the press of those years defines electronic or e-commerce), for banking and to read the "Miami Herald" or the "New York Times" before it hits newsstands in the morning. The service costs $600 for the terminal, $12 per month and $1 per hour for the telephone connection. According to the chronicles of the time, banking services are few (access to the current account and a little more) and so inefficient as to cause a rapid abandonment by many users. In March 1986, after just under two and a half years of life, with $50 million in losses and only 5,000 customers, Viewtron closes.

In that period, other services similar to those proposed by Videofinancial Services take shape: the Gateway of Times Mirror (1984, closed in March 1986), Trintex (joint venture of CBS with IBM and Sears), CNR (Citicorp, RCA and Nynex) and others, mostly closed since 1986.

In the same article of the New York Times already quoted, a prophecy: «My feeling says William Moroney, president of the Electronic Funds Transfer Association (EFTA) is that 1983 will see an explosion in domestic financial services. But the market won't mature until kids who grew up using computers go to college and start earning enough to think about saving. And a large part of what is at stake is linked to the technological developments between now and that moment ». Seldom was a prediction more accurate.

Meanwhile, in 1981 Norddeutsche Teilzahlungkreditbank (NTB) became the first European bank to have started an electronic current account management service. German from Hamburg, she was born in 1955 and has been active in the online sector since 1975 with the subsidiary Verbraucherbank, also known as the Consumer Bank (English translation of its German name, which indicates a bank focused on private customers). NTB's history is tied to its name, which roughly means "North German Consumer Credit Bank", a type of specialized bank that was suppressed in 1986.

As early as 1975, NTB was perhaps the first fully computerized German bank, but this technological effort was initially aimed mainly inwards with the aim of reducing the costs associated with the process of processing information and requests from branches. The architect of the Hamburg technological revolution is the pioneer and CEO of NTB, as well as cellist, Alfred Richter, who in mid-1976 illustrates to the press the plans for the future of the bank on the basis of the newly built infrastructure: "Banks today look like grocery stores he stigmatized and data processing is mostly used today as an information system. Our goal, on the other hand, is to create a bank in three years in which the services are not carried out by human hands ".

Richter does some math: a rented mainframe costs him 1 million marks a year, which is the average cost of 50 employees. But without this tool, he would have to have 120 employees to get the same results. And if the costs of the connection lines between the offices and the branches are another 250,000,000 marks a year, these are practically in balance with the savings obtained thanks to fewer employee movements, the optimization of resources and the reduction of errors of processing. "With credit checks adds Richter we save at least 1 million a year". Errors and delays also cost banks about 1.5% of profits, but Richter with technology aims to bring this figure down to 0.8%. At the end of 1975, NTB had 133 employees, lent 300 million marks a year and had branches in Berlin, Bremen, Düsseldorf, Duisburg, Frankfurt, Hanover, Cologne and Lübeck, all electronically connected to the Hamburg headquarters. The mainframe on which the whole structure is based, the "machine", is an IBM 370/135 with 384 Kb of main memory; each operator at the head office can access a total of 380,000 customer accounts from IBM 3277 workstations, while IBM 3275 terminals are available in branch offices for remote verification. The software that manages the operations was developed internally at the bank by Richter and his team. From 7am to 11pm, the bank can then automatically process loans, credit risk management, payments, taxes, and external communications.

The system is also facilitated by the fact that the majority of customers repay the loan installments with postal bills; therefore, the post office sends the data to the bank in the form of magnetic tapes, from which it can easily transfer the data to its computers.

In 1979 Verbraucherbank, which is preparing to introduce a new mainframe, the IBM 4341, recorded the opening of 12,000 accounts, which in 1980 became 30,000 and in 1981 45,000. Excellent growth, due to the radical approach of "do-it-yourself bank" (in German SB-bank, i.e., Selbstbedienung Bank).

The branches are in fact equipped with terminals made available free of charge to customers, who can thus manage numerous operations on their own. To do this, they have a card with a magnetic stripe that they must insert into a reader, then dial a keyword on the keyboard. It is thus possible to monitor the performance of securities, check interest rates, make transfers, and wire transfers and more. According to Richter, in 1981 86% of the bank's transactions took place from SB (self-service) terminals in the branch and of these 60% were carried out on weekends or in the evening, in any case outside office hours, in automated branches obviously open to the public even at unusual times. But 1981 was the real turning point for Verbraucherbank. It was in fact in that year that the experimentation phase of the local version of Videotex, the BTX, was launched in Germany, involving for the moment the areas of Düsseldorf and Berlin. Here, thanks to the work of the IT manager of the Hamburg institute, Peter Koehn, about 2,000 bank customers test the online services from their home by connecting the Datasaab terminal, rented or bought in a post office, to the domestic telephone; even if the official launch of the BTX will take place only two years later, the birth of German home banking can nevertheless be considered this.

Through Videotex, customers obtain general information on the bank, on the services and on the due dates of the accounts and instalments to be paid, or to switch to the current account management service. For almost all functions the normal simplified keyboard of the terminal is sufficient; however, for more complex services (including sending electronic communications to the bank) an additional keyboard costing 300 marks is required.

In 1985 Verbraucherbank-Consumer Bank, with 50,000 declared users, received the enthusiastic definition of "the world's most popular service" from the international press. In 1986 it will be taken over by Noris Bank and will begin a long history of ownership changes. Shortly after the first pioneers, heavyweights take to the field in the United States, in the form of four big New York banks (Chemical Bank in September 1982, Chase Manhattan Bank, Manufacturers Hanover Bank and Citibank in December 1984, the first three later merged into JP Morgan Chase), a Californian credit institution (Bank of America, December 1983) and a broker (EF Hutton, whom we will meet later), who set up an online current account management service through Videotex.

Chemical Bank, which in 1995 will be the third largest bank in the United States, presented itself on the market with the service called Pronto, initially given in tests to 200 customers of the New York headquarters: based precisely on Videotext, for 2 dollars per month becomes the first home banking service in the US by number of customers, about 21,000 in 1985, out of the bank's 1,150,000 total customers. The number, as we can see, remains proportionally limited, once again due to the high costs of use, and is essentially a failure compared to management's expectations.

Pronto allows you to pay bills, transfer funds, see your checking account balance, work out family budgets, and track your checks. Chemical will progressively offer its service to other banks throughout the country and will then introduce a version of the service dedicated to small businesses. The Pronto pilot project was developed starting in 1982 with an investment of 20 million dollars and will close in 1989 with a loss of about 30 million dollars.

Citibank's Home Base for $10 a month offers the same services as Pronto, plus Dow Jones NIS news and data for an additional $10.

Figure 13 • The logo of the Chemical Bank (USA) home banking service in 1985

In the same period, Bank of America reported about 17,000 customers for its online current account management service based on Videotex technology, Homebanking, accessible from any computer; with it it is possible to transfer funds, manage and monitor current accounts and checks and pay the bills of hundreds of affiliated companies. All for $8 a month and with no connection costs.
Chase Manhattan Bank's Spectrum service also combines online banking with trading, through the group's discount broker, Dahlman Rose & Co.; the service is available for IBM compatible, Apple II or Commodore 64 and offers online payment of bills and checks, e-mail and updates on bank rates; for an additional 5 dollars a month it is possible to trade online (but other specific services were already born), to receive the prices of the securities and the performance of the indices.
At the same time, the home banking Homelink, based on Prestel, was born in 1983 from the collaboration between Bank of Scotland and Nottingham Building Society (NBS). It is no coincidence that it was developed and provided to users by a financial company emanating from a group active

in construction: in those years, in fact, the large English construction companies are becoming dangerous competi-

Figure 14 • An advertisement for Chase Manhattan Bank's Spectrum home banking service (1985)

tors of traditional banks due to the large flows of capital they manage. and the financial services they offer to their clients; the banks then try to bring them back under their control with agreements, partnerships, and stock exchanges. With Homelink, bills could be paid online, and it was possible to transfer money to the Bank of Scotland and then withdraw them from local ATMs.

Telematization of private banking services rapidly spreads and other European banks follow suit: Götabanken in Gothenburg (Sweden), the Glaskow (Scotland) branch of TSB (United Kingdom) in 1985, then Barclays, Lloyds Bank, Rabobank and gradually many others until meeting, as repeatedly reiterated, with the launch pad called the Internet which, alongside the unsuccessful marketing policies, will also be the decisive factor that will lead to the extinction, within a few years, of the attempted invasion of USA by the European (Franco-British) technology of Videotex. In 1985 The Gartner Group released an optimistic research according to which the US market of Videotex from 4 billion dollars will increase to 32 billion in 1990.

In August 1985, however, the magazine "Communications News" laconically notes that "public services Videotex languish" and the situation, ultimately, will not change.

The fate of the tone telephone (with keypad, technically defined as "Dual-Tone Multi-Frequency" or DTMF) is different, which will progressively replace the pulse one (disk) and which is now present in all homes; the invention dates back to the 1960s and is a US Western Electric patent marketed by Bell System under the name of Touch-Tone.

AT&T was the first telecom to adopt it for its customers in November 1963. Other companies later developed similar products, such as Nortel Networks' Digitone; among its first applications we find the combination with interactive services for cable television customers and the Autovon, a military telephone system suppressed in the 1990s. Widespread starting from the late '70s, the Touch-Tone and its countless imitations will become the hallmark of modern telephony starting from 1984. That is when in the USA the giant AT&T, now a de facto monopolist, will be dismembered into many regional companies (called "baby Bell", compared to the parent company called "Ma Bell") to encourage competition. This will mark the birth of a myriad of new telephone-digital services based on customer interaction with keypad phones, useful for entering credit card numbers and passwords, accessing bank accounts, placing financial orders and more.

But well before the boom, a few years after the launch of the Touch-Tone on the market, many banks have adopted it precisely to allow customers the first rudimentary automated current account management. Among the first, Bank of Delaware, which provides a primitive service both via keyboard and via automatic responder which can be addressed with a vocabulary of 64 words. It will not be long before it will be possible to trade financial stocks with the touch-tone phone. According to reports from the Canadian-US online broker TD Ameritrade on its website, the first service of this type was launched in 1988 by its subsidiary Accutrade under the name of Touchtone Telephone Trading. Born in 1975 on the wave of the explosion of the discount broker sector (due, as already mentioned, to the end of the NYSE monopoly on admission fees to stock market trading), Ameritrade was founded by Joe Rickett with the name of First Omaha; in 1987 it became TransTerra (headed by Accutrade) and only in 1997, after the acquisition of the pioneer K. Aufhauser & Co. in 1995 and then of eBroker, will it take the name it will keep even after its integration into the Canadian banking group Toronto Dominion and will enter the online trading business via the Internet. Accutrade's (or AccuTrade) tone telephone trading service initially costs 3 cents per share traded with a minimum of $48 per order. To cite only one example among many, Quick & Reilly, a small company founded in 1974 in Palm Beach, Florida, and initially made up of only four people, grew by being the first to offer telephone services with a 40% discount compared to the previous market average. Q&R (now incorporated into Bank of America) will be followed in 1989 by Charles Schwab & Co. with a similar service. As J. Chritopher Westland and Theodor HK Clark wrote in 1999, "Discount brokers enter the electronic brokerage market gradually because they have to consider the effect of giving credibility to the emerging market that is accelerating customer migration. Schwab and Fidelity first experiment with touch tone trading by offering a 10% discount on commissions over traditional trading.

The discount then extends to executed orders sent through the proprietary front-end software that allows access to financial intermediaries via modem. The touch-tone telephone, in short, is only the starter of real online trading, whose subsequent developments will lead to the addition of a video, a wider headboard and a hundredfold processing capacity to the digitized telephone line and the telephone set. with Videotex first and then with the PC. An appetizer, however, that we have not finished eating yet, given that this type of access to the markets is still alive and well, offered by a large number of online brokers who use it today mainly as an emergency channel next to the call center.

With the development of technology and networks, the step towards real home banking is only a matter of time, but the development will come after the birth of the Web in 1994.

Also in this case, as in the previous ones, it will initially be made available only the informative part of the account, not the dispositive part, which will arrive in the following years. From this moment on, however, we abandon home banking in the USA, which will follow its own path (even if repeatedly destined to intersect with trading) but which remains a different service for a different type of clientele. While in fact the vast majority of people have a current account to manage (obviously I am referring to Western companies) and are interested in investing and protecting their savings, only a small minority is ready to risk their capital in part or entirely by trading securities. financial and even less are those among them who have the ability, the will, and the resources to do it online. Nor can it be said, as we shall see, that home banking is, technologically or ideally, the precursor of trading. Rather, they are two different services developed in parallel based on technologies created to telematize interbank financial transactions at national and international level.

Online services and finance

At the end of the 1960s, the first online commercial services were developed that exploit the nascent technology of time-sharing, or the possibility for multiple users to share the resources of a computer on the network. Born at Dartmouth College in Hanover (New Hampshire, USA) on May 1st, 1964, time-sharing is developed to reduce the management costs of company computers without affecting the performance of the single machine; from the commercial services that are based on it, the giants of online services of the 1990s and 2000s will arise and only the spread of ADSL will reduce its importance in favor of the large national telecoms. On these premises in 1969 the first CompuServe online services company was born in Columbus, Ohio, founded by an insurance company that, having acquired the PDP-10 computers made by DEC, realized that they were oversized compared to its needs. For this reason, he decided to make them available for payment to other companies through the time-sharing method.

The peculiarity of CompuServe is that it immediately designs and builds all the infrastructure, including hardware and software, on its own. By deploying its computers throughout the United States and then to other parts of the world over the years (in Europe since 1982), CompuServe creates a relatively low-cost (around $30 per hour) network accessible anywhere via telephone and modem. It is a network based on a packet switching protocol developed in-house and which will subsequently be integrated with the most modern protocol evolutions.

It gradually adds specific content to connection, memory, and processing capacity. In 1978 the CompuServe Information Service (CIS) service for individuals was launched which from 1989 will provide access to the World Wide Web and e-mails; in 1987 the CIS will be worth 50% of the group's turnover.

However, one of the most profitable services is managed by the Financial Services Division, which provides financial data from a large number of sources starting from stock exchanges and private databases, and then develops its own systems for selecting and analyzing securities. which will soon be used by all major investment banks (CompuStat and others). Becoming a small Internet network ante litteram able to provide all kinds of services to users, both directly and through thousands of companies that progressively enter into agreements with CompuServe, it is inevitable that many financial companies also choose this service as a showcase and mass distribution channel.

In its early years, CompuServe's only real competitor will be The Source. Founded in 1979 in McLean, Virginia, by Bill von Meister and Jack Taub, the company will quickly move towards the creation of information services accesssible through users' microcomputers, which are becoming increasingly popular, at low cost.

The service was launched in June of the same year and at its presentation the science fiction writer Isaac Asimov will comment that it is the birth of the information age ("the start of the information age"). Subsequently numerous other online information services will be born, among which the best known are Delphi, founded by Wes Kussmaul in 1981 (but active since 1982); among the numerous changes of hands (the last occurred on 11 September 2011) Delphi recorded the acquisition by News Corporation of Rupert Murdoch in 1993, which then sold it to a company formed by some of the previous shareholders. The management of NewsCo has in fact seen the number of users plummet from 125,000 in 1995 to a few tens of thousands in 1996. The importance of Delphi lies in the fact that it will be the first commercial service ever to use the TCP I IP communication protocol.

CompuServe, The Source and Delphi will host many companies and services related to the world of finance within their systems.

In 1983 the great rival of CompuServe, America On Line (AOL, also strongly focused on private services), will be born, which will undermine it from its leading position and which in 1997 will take over the same CompuServe. In 1984 the future giant Prodigy will be born, while in 1985 it will be the turn of Genie, the online service of General Electric, which will be active until 1994 and which will gather 350,000 users.

Except for CompuServe, most of the commercial online services use transmission protocols based on X25 encoding, the same which, as we have seen, is used in France for the Minitel network (1982) and in Italy for the Itapac network, created by SIP (Telecom Italia, today) starting from 1986. In short, between the 1950s and the early 1970s, the information technology industry took a great leap forward, supported by a growing activity of marketing of the first expensive products and services almost exclusively directed towards medium-sized organizations and big companies, the only subjects able to bear the disproportionate costs of the first bulky infrastructures and having complex needs for processing large quantities of data and for transmission to decentralized offices, sometimes scattered across continents. However, starting from the 1980s, the rapid spread of personal computers and microcomputers (starting from large and medium-sized companies and then to private individuals) allowed manufacturers to accumulate sufficient capital to free themselves from defense funding, invest in research and development and reduce the prices of products making them accessible to the public, starting a virtuous spiral that has not stopped since then.

The computerization of the markets

However, having a technological intermediary is not enough if the stock exchanges are not. The steps necessary to put the trader in contact with the markets are in fact numerous and each of them requires an ad hoc channel and for all the channels of the financial chain to be telematized it will take many years. Simplifying a lot, the trader connects to his internet connection provider, which connects him to the web and from there to his online broker; this in turn is connected to the exchanges (both for the execution of orders and for the provision of data) and to other online service providers (news, data processing, etc.) the exchange in turn is connected to the service providers of clearing and settlement. Even today, all this path is not fully telematized in any case. Meanwhile, not all world stock exchanges are, and this not only due to lack of resources but also for "political" needs. The most sensational and current case is that of the NYSE: its system of negotiation of the auction with shouts (i.e., with voice negotiation requests in special rooms) has been for years strenuously defended by the operators who work there, both for fear of being replaced by computers and for the belief that the presence of expert personnel who interrupts the flow of orders and is able to assess their relevance for the market can reduce the risk of dramatic events for the whole system.

For this reason, only since 1995 has the connection between brokers and professionals present in the NYSE trading rooms and that between the latter and the market been digitized, thus maintaining the presence of the operators themselves as a human element of connection (or interruption). of the two streams. Professionals, however, can choose how to operate within a hybrid system: let the order run automatically or manage it manually; in fact, the automatic flow has levels, called "liquidity replenishment points" (LPR), at which manual trading is automatically triggered, interrupting the digitized one; in this way the market is slowed down, and the presence of operators reduces (or should reduce) the risks of excessively sudden price changes. Even within brokers, digitization has never been total. In the 1980s and 1990s, in many cases the order that arrives online from the private client appears on the terminal of a trader at the trading desk (i.e., on the computer of the professional who works in the intermediary's offices) who sends it to the market with different methods (telephone, fax, e-mail, computer) and often confirms the order even after a few hours. This is because, aside from NASDAQ, the markets are not yet equipped to take orders over the Internet.

Even today, some apparently online markets, such as Forex (for which "market" is an improper definition), have two people on the phone at the end of the supply chain who negotiate the exchange price by voice. This is because since these are OTC (over-the-counter, i.e., unregulated) markets, there are no specific rules to be respected in negotiations. In many cases, individual institutions, or groups of them have set up private alternative circuits in which to exchange bonds, currencies, CFDs and other securities online, but these are however limited initiatives.

Parallel to the spread of online trading (in this case intended as a connection with the broker only), driven by the success of NASDAQ and ECNs, both in the United States and as we will see in Europe, even the "shouts" are becoming more and more feeble, to give way to the muffled sound of keyboard clicks. This is because the stock exchanges also initiate a telematic process to reduce costs, negotiation times but also the high number of errors that the cries have always brought with them.

Leaving aside the NASDAQ, born in 1971 already based on an exclusively telematic model, in North America a list claims the primacy of the first regulated telematic stock market on a razor's edge with the NASDAQ (which, we recall, was born as an electronic list of OTC securities and only in 1975 did it become a fully-fledged stock exchange). This is the Cincinnnati Stock Exchange, now transformed into the National Stock Exchange, which in 1976 will definitively close the floor (the trading room) to replace it with a fully automated system. Gradually, stock exchanges and ECNs from the United States, then from Europe and Asia, but also from Latin America, quickly enter the digital highway. The London Stock Exchange started digitization starting from

1988, while in Italy, the Milan Stock Exchange became completely telematic in 1997, after having absorbed all the other Italian stock exchanges and having taken on the name of Borsa Italiana. The bag automation process is not yet complete, and it is not certain that it will ever be. However, the main world-wide regulated lists are easily accessible through online trading services.

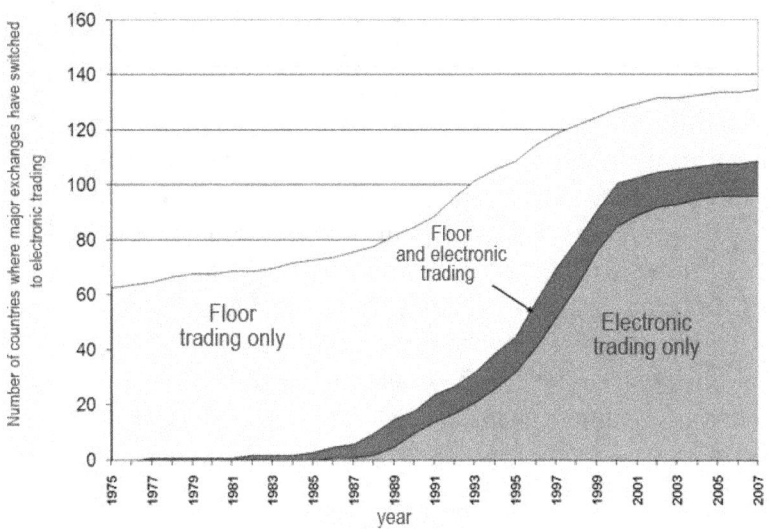

Figure 15 • The evolution of world stock exchanges from trading "to shouts" to electronic trading

Furthermore, technology also in this case favors the reduction of costs and therefore competition. For this reason, to do but a few examples, in 1992 Chicago Mercantile Exchange (CME), Singapore International Monetary Exchange (Simex) and the French Matif joined together and launched Globex, a regulated electronic market for derivatives and options; the following year the New York Mercantile Exchange (Nymex) opens in London an electronic access service to its market of contracts relating to the energy sector and over the following years the technology pervasively invades the most important lists in the world. Which, in addition to digitizing exchanges, connect with each other: CME and LIFFE (London International Financial Futures & Options Exchange), for example, integrate their respective derivatives trading platforms, Globex 2 and Liffe Connect.

Until 2011, when two so-called MTFs (multilateral trading facilities, a form of regulated exchange created within the European Union), the British Chi-X and the European branch of the American Bats, merge to give life to the third world pole in terms of trading volumes after that of NYSE Euronext (a merger in turn of the US market and the European circuit which includes the Paris, Brussels and Amsterdam stock exchanges) and that of NASDAQ OMX (consisting of the North American list and the Scandinavian stock exchange circuit).

CHAPTER 2

The 1980s and the first generation of online brokers

From the early 1970s, the US Defense opened the Arpanet computer network to private individuals, which in 1982 officially became the Internet, while in 1976 the newborn Apple, founded by the two seventeen-year-olds Steve Jobs and Steve Wozniak, presented the Apple I computer; in 1977 the company, which takes its name from the famous apple that would have stimulated Newton to study gravity (reported in the original brand of the company), launched the Apple II and in the 1980s the Apple III. In 1981 IBM launched the Personal Computer 5150, which from that moment will become the "pc" by definition, will invade offices all over the world and will become a world standard. After the birth of Instinet in 1969, the liberalization of the US financial market in 1975 and the birth of the NASDAQ in 1972, it is 1982 that marks another important step towards the electronic trading of listed financial securities for individuals, or online trading. In April of that year, in fact, Max Ule & Co., a broker controlled by the New York financial company Rosenkrantz, Ehrenkrants, Lyon & Ross Inc., launched Tickerscreen, a BBS (bulletin board system, forerunner of current online forums) which makes available to users the closing prices of the NYSE, the closing of the indexes and a system of comparison with the costs of competing services. The free system is directly competitive with that provided for a fee by giants such as Dow Jones.

The company, which bears the name of its founder and president, also makes available to users the Tickertec software with which it is possible to carry out analyzes on market data received with a delay of 15 minutes, but with costs already prohibitive at the time: from 1,000 to $6,975 depending on configurations. Within a few weeks, the service will expand to direct trading of securities in the "after hours" (evening market): the customer sends the order which is taken over by the desk and sent to the market the next morning.

It is not yet "real time" nor online trading in the modern sense, but it is an important first step. The name "Tickerscreen" has been registered since July 1979, a sign that Max Ule's ideas have long been waiting for technology and capital to meet. Max Ule himself, in an interview carried out at the time of the launch of the initiative, says that the idea would come to him thinking of the fact that he had three computers and three telephone lines that remained completely unused at night. "I hope this is the way to intercept a new type of customer he says the type of businessman who spends 80% of his time in meetings, who is a computer expert and who owns a PC through which to enter the orders". And for those who don't have a pc, he wants to make an agreement with a manufacturer to supply them at a discounted price. A profile of Max Ule's career can be found on his personal website, which appears to have been abandoned for some time. After having worked in the marketing of a financial company and having become the director and major shareholder of a Cleveland brokerage, Ule leads a division of Rosenkrantz and associates (the one that will create Tickerscreen), then he is appointed vice president of another financial company, to move to Herzog Heine Geduld (now incorporated into Bank of America) under the label of "Max Ule Division". Eventually, he became Vice President of Investments at Shields & Company, after which his professional traces were lost. The story of Max Ule, however, is intertwined with that of Trade*Plus, a company that years later will be at the basis of the development of a world giant in the sector and which could rightly be considered the first real online trading service of the generation of the Years. '80 or pre-Internet. However, the conditional is a must, since NAICO-Net is also competing for the primacy, as we will see later. In 1982, in fact, fifty-two years old physicist and inventor William Porter and his contemporary Bernard Newcomb, founded the Trade*Plus company in Palo Alto, California, with $15,000 of initial capital. The two met at a party in 1980 and Newcomb (nearly blind since birth and a three-year employee in General Electric's data processing service) has just bought himself an Apple II. Porter then involves his friend in his plan to use the computer to obtain and manage stock quotes, bypassing the costly intermediaries and traditional data providers. The first online service offered by Trade*Plus is based on Max Ule's Tickerscreen software. Porter, however, does not stop there. His idea is that in a few years it will be possible to see in every office work stations with PCs equipped with modems, therefore used by potential customers of online services, and that in the financial world the commissions then around 9% per transaction in the brokerage traditional have large margins for reduction.

Porter builds, for and in collaboration with broker CD Anderson & Co., a new automated order entry system that is made available to CD Anderson clients in July 1983 under the name Desk Top Broker. And on July 11, 1983, a dentist from Michigan (United States) goes down in history for being the first private user in the world to place online orders directly on the stock exchange. Trade*Plus, therefore, is initially not an online broker, but rather an IT company that builds trading systems for the financial sector.

Desk Top Broker allows you to send orders online to the CD Anderson desk and have them confirmed in a period of time that can vary from 90 seconds to 15 minutes. The execution is then confirmed by e-mail with automatic updating of the portfolio; Market orders are available, with limits, valid until cancelled and daily, stop-loss, stop-buy, and stop-sell orders, while it is possible to use margins and short selling. Desk Top Broker offers prices updated in real time or delayed by 20 minutes, the ability to monitor the orders of the last year and the prices of 18 securities simultaneously and to activate sound alarms in case of exceeding the limits entered. The software can then be integrated with Lotusplan 1-2-3, Multiplan or Visicalc for personal data processing and allows the entry of open market orders and the management of the securities portfolio. The costs, however, for home users are still high: $195 for signing up to the Trade*Plus contract, $15 per month for one hour of connection, $24 per hour for connecting to open markets, and $6 at closed markets; for real-time data, individuals pay $75 a month, professionals $135, as determined by the NASD. It cannot be said that Desk Top Broker is an astonishing success: after 18 months of activity, approximately 500 customers will have subscri-bed to the service.

Hard to say whether Trade*Plus or CD Anderson ranks as the first online broker in history. In fact, between 1982 and 1983 the two companies remain closely linked, the first as a supplier and manager of the electronic trading system (but not as a financial intermediary), the second as a financial company that offers it to its customers and which, in after all, he puts his face to it.

Founded in San Francisco by C. Derek Anderson, he started a service in 1983 that by 1984 will lead him to have 500 online customers, who will guarantee 12% of the company's revenue. Born in 1941 in Los Angeles, Derek Anderson began his career in finance working at the Pacific Stock Exchange and for some small financial firms; in 1973 he founded the company that bears his name, "one of the first discount brokers in America he himself states in an interview and the first to offer investments online, ten years too soon". After the sale in 1985 of the assets to Security Pacific Banks (now integrated into Bank of America), Anderson will give life to the investment company Plantagenet Capital, named after a dynasty, that has given at least 15 kings to England and from which he boasts to descend. As of mid-1984, the exclusivity agreement between Trade*Plus and CD Andersen having expired, Porter will be free to sell its technology service to other financial intermediaries, banks and traditional brokers wishing to go online. The service quickly became popular among financial companies and will be adopted, among others, by Quick & Reilly (which uses it to manage online customers of the Chemical Bank Pronto service), by Charles Schwab (similarly connected with Bank of America), by Fidelity Investments (for the service called Investor's Express), Texas Securities and others. Only later, as we will see, will Porter found E*Trade with its own online trading service destined to revolutionize the market and make its group a point of reference worldwide. Almost simultaneously the North American Holding Corporation (NAH) of East Hartford (Connecticut), led by Edward M. Kopko, launches the NAICO-Net service through its subsidiary North American Investment Corp. (NAICO). The testimony of the American trader, writer and trainer Natalie Stetz Tobias, does not seem to leave doubts about the astonishment caused by the novelty: "I remember the first time I saw in my Radio Shack [shop of a US computer chain, NdA] a computer with black screen and fluorescent green lettering. It was 1981. But already a year later, in 1982, the first complete trading service for private users was put online to buy and sell stocks, mutual funds and commodities using a PC. It was called NAICO-Net and was offered by a company called North American Holding Corporation based in East Hartford, Connecticut.

The system was based on ANSI coding, that is, it used terminals, but IBM PCs could connect to it through a simple application from anywhere in the world. Orders were being sent directly to the Pershing Corporation of the Donaldson Lufkin & Jenrette (DLJ) group for high-speed clearing and the number of traders had rapidly grown to around 5,000". NAICO-Net can be accessed through the connection services provided by Delphi, CompuServe, and The Source. Compared to the competition, NAICO-Net also provides customers with a research service and stock market operational indications on shares followed by an internal desk of analysts, in addition to not requesting payment for any share at the time of subscription and charging only the services used during the online connection. "And NAICONet underlines a magazine of the time, Inc. Magazine charges a slightly lower commission than other full-service intermediaries".

North American Holding listed on the NASDAQ in March 1984, offering one million shares, and rising from approximately $2 million to nearly $18 million in revenue, according to data reported on the New York Times website and PR Newswire. and profits of $500,000 in 1987. The vice-president for the telecom area of NAICO (whose name could not be recovered), attributes the authorship of the NAICO-Net project, which he would have developed starting from the spring of 1983 and which he defines as "the first system electronic securities exchange for individuals to buy and sell shares, mutual funds and commodities with a PC or terminal". NAICO-Net would have reached 5,000 customers within a few years, subsequently developing for the telecommunications giant MCI (now Verizon) the interactive information service Insight, based on telex and on the integration of about 400 databases, of which about 200 financial.

An advertisement of the time, featured in the weekly "InfoWorld" of 28 July 1986, announces the revolution in online communication, offered through the company Networked System International (NSI, controlled by North American Investments): the first teleconferencing system via pc and telex to the world, in collaboration with MCI, a large database of over 4,200 over-thecounter companies and securities (OTC News Alert), created with Comtex and the "NASD Board of Governors", and the NAICO-Net service.

«Trade securities online with NAICO-Net says the advertisement your direct line with a unique brokerage service worldwide. Via pc or telex, you can 'call your broker' at any time, day, or night. Open a personal or business account to receive discounted commissions for trading stocks 'online'» (quotes are in the original).

The service is provided through the Tymnet and Uninet networks, with connection costs ranging from 6 to 27 dollars per hour depending on the speed chosen (from 110 to 2,400 baud), or in dial-up, i.e., through the normal telephone network, $1 to $3 per hour; no connection costs for telex access. The idea is innovative and, like CD Anderson's, potentially disruptive.

However, disaster is just around the corner, a disaster that for the North American Holding group is named after Joseph P. McGivney. The reconstruction of the facts is complex, but in essence it is a sensational case of multilevel marketing in which the management of the group is more or less consciously involved.

McGivney is in fact a financial planner (a financial promoter) with an extraordinary charisma, an immense chutzpah, and a great desire to make money without going too far. In short, a great seller who would be able to sell ice to the Eskimos. In 1981, at the age of 47, he started his business by spreading the "word" in Bridgeview, a suburb of Chicago. It does so through meetings open to growing crowds, called "Wealth Unlimited Seminar", in which on the one hand it enhances the financial risk and investments in OTC shares of companies characterized by great "potential" for growth, on the other it proposes to those who he listens to become not only the buyer, but himself the seller of the financial proposals from his creation, JPM Industries, where obviously JPM are the initials of his name and the company is little more than an empty box. One of his favorite phrases is: «Our fathers taught us to put money in the bank, to never make investments and not to take risks. In this way, only the banks got rich».

His initial activity, in fact, is limited to sales preparation courses for the company and the dissemination of information material relating to the company itself, from which, within a couple of years, he will receive 4.2 million dollars. His overwhelming oratorical art and the successes of the early years attracted what a newspaper of the time called "suburban masses" (we are on the outskirts of one of the most industrialized cities in the United States), made up of students, workers and artisans who hardly made it to end of the month and who are proudly nicknamed "Joe-workhards", meaning hard-working average Americans.

McGivney's number of salespeople-customers reaches 14,000; it makes them buy (and incentivize to sell) shares of unlisted companies: that of JPMI itself, but also those of the Hospital Newspapers Group, of UAS Automation Systems and, coincidentally, that of North American Ventures (NAV) of East Hartford, Connecticut.

Here, then, is the first knot of the plot between McGivney and the Kopko brothers. Edward (31 years old in 1987), president of NAICO, has in fact a younger brother, Frederick, lawyer and major shareholder of an important Chicago firm, D'Ancona&Pflaum, but also director of NAH (the parent company), of NAICO (the broker controlled by NAH) and of North American Ventures (NAV, investment finance company), as well as being the solicitor of JPMI and numerous companies whose shares McGivney offers around Illinois. The close bond between Frederick Kopko and Joseph McGivney is then evident when, on July 1st, 1985, JPMI is quoted on the NASDAQ; from this operation

NAICO (which in addition to being an online broker also carries out traditional financial activities, such as bringing companies that need capital to the stock market) obtains 250,000 dollars and 30,000 shares of JPMI thanks to the role of "independent qualified subscriber".

A definition that for the NASD has a very specific meaning in relation to the correctness of the pre-listing due diligence. A fairness which, given the evident conflict of interest of its directors, could not be guaranteed. Also, because McGivney does not include in the prospectus the links with the NAH group, which will subsequently be an active market maker of JPMI as well as of all the proposed companies that will come to go public.

However, the market seems enthusiastic about this company and values it $470 million, against a 1986 turnover of 8 million and a profit (the first in its history) of around $400,000. Meanwhile, at the end of 1986 North American Ventures acquires Butler International (active in the aircraft equipment sector, a sector that Frederick Kopko follows as a lawyer) which in 1992 will give its name to the whole group; on January 6, 1988, NAICO takes over the assets of the investment bank Providence Securities.

On May 10, 1988, Butler-NAICO filed a lawsuit against the clearing company Donaldson Lufkin & Jenrette asking for more than $100 million in damages for irregular practices, but thus initiating a negative spiral that will lead to July 5 to the suspension of brokerage operations and July 7 to the sale of the brokerage business to private clients and their accounts to the New York broker Jonathan Alan & Co. (founded in 1983 and taken over by the Titan Values group in 1990). It does not appear that neither Alan first nor Titan then carried out NAICO's online activities. On July 18, 1988, the information branch of the company,

Networking and World Information, was then sold. That's the end of the online and NAICO-Net activities.

Finally, in February 1990, Joseph McGivney, the D'Ancona & Pflaum law firm (i.e., Frederick Kopko), Edward Kopko and others are placed under investigation by a Connecticut federal judge, the first to have sold shares in unlisted companies without license, the others for "manipulation of securities, unauthorized promotion and sale of shares on customer accounts, excessive mark-up on securities, parking of securities in customer accounts, improper use of margins", all causing, according to the prosecution of the District Attorney, "millions of dollars in losses to thousands of customers." How the case ended matters little but suffice it to say that in the following years we will find Edward M. Kopko directing a magazine for business executives and his brother practicing as a lawyer at another firm.

The NAH group, which became Butler International and disposed of the financial activities first and then the aeronautical ones, will focus on various IT and engineering services and then go into bankruptcy in 2009, selling part of the activities to Butler America, still active, consisting of some former senior executives.

A world in turmoil

We have therefore arrived at July 1984, when the journalist Jim Bartimo, taking stock of the situation of online trading in the United States, describes in the US magazine "InfoWorld", in the article entitled "Clients with micro-computers challenge financial intermediaries", a world in turmoil: of the approximately 75-80,000 financial intermediaries active in the United States, 10% that is, 7-8,000 companies use microcomputers to offer their services, with an expected increase of 30% for 1985.

In 1984, therefore, approximately 520,000 customers actively connect to the microcomputers that the approximately 8,000 brokers have. In the vast majority of cases, these are discount brokers, "discount" intermediaries who offer online services to monitor information and accounts (and which only in very few cases allow the electronic sending of orders), but not analyses or research, which therefore user has to do it himself; to do this, brokers provide stock market data in real time (which in those days means with many seconds of delay, at best) or deferred by 15-20 minutes, but also information databases that are always updated and have been available for some time. in digital format and which will have a huge development up to the present day. Among these are those of Dow Jones, The Source and dozens of others, which collectively represent a cornerstone of the development of modern online trading, and which will give way to decades of controversy both about the opportunity for a private client to make their own choices of investment without the assistance of specialized professionals, both due to the influence they have and will increasingly have on a large mass of investors (professionals and individuals) and on their ability to change market trends. The strong diffusion of online trading progressively pushes the large online services such as CompuServe and The Source, which earn on users' time spent on the network, to enter into agreements with new telematic brokers to further increase the traffic that passes through their systems, offering to users connection and access to large amounts of information and third-party services, and to brokers of the huge and crowded "virtual squares" on which to go and offer their products. The activism of online services in recruiting "traffic generators" will therefore lead in a few years (before the general confluence on the Web) to the division of online brokers into two categories: those active through online services and those with direct connection. For many years, however, the development of the sector will be delayed by the high connection fees (calculated precisely by time), generally higher than those of the trading fees.

For this reason, all services offer the function of preparing orders off-line to then enter them in a few seconds after connection. In September 1984, still according to "InfoWorld", Delphi offers NAICO-Net for $19.95, CompuServe has been connected to Max Ule (who already has 175 customers) for three weeks, growing at the rate of three to five new accounts opened every day, while CD Anderson declares that already 10-15% of its business (started the previous year) passes through the Desk Top Brokers online trading service. In the same month The Source announces the launch, within a few weeks, of its online trading service, Investor Services or Executive Investor Services, managed by Spear Securities of Los Angeles and which will cost $18.5 per month for stock market data (New York, American Stock Exchange, and OTC) in real time; the system constantly updates all data after each order, including taxes.

In 1994, at the dawn of the World Wide Web, among the brokers still connected to online services we will find Pershing on Prodigy, E*Trade, Quick & Reilly and Max Ule Investments on CompuServe, Trade*Plus and Quick & Reilly on America On Line, while among the "direct" Pidelity Investments (via Tymnet), Charles Schwab and Accutrade. It should be noted that E*Trade and Trade*Plus belong to the same shareholders. In September 1984 Spear Securities of Los Angeles, led by Richard Smiley and controlled by Spear Financial Services headed by Charles (Chuck) Spear, also entered the fray on The Source; in March 1985 it will collect 700 online customers, to reach 5,000 two years later. To trade stocks, you need to subscribe to The Source ($49.95 one-time), while the connection cost varies from 14 to 46 cents per minute ($8-27 per hour), with a minimum of $10 per month.

Spear, which has an agreement with NEC for the sale of computers at discounted prices to users, offers stock market data delayed by 15 minutes, allows trading on about a thousand stocks, and allows you to have a confirmation of the execution within two minutes of sending. In January 1984 The Source claims that "more than 1,200 traders" have signed up for Spear's service. The platform ("which gives access to market parterres throughout the United States") allows you to select the desired markets and securities or to take advantage of a list of 200 pre-selected stocks and options. Furthermore, the negotiations carried out are recorded and the taxes to be paid calculated and then automatically saved on a printable file that reproduces the document to be presented to the tax authorities, the model D. It is then in October 1984 the announcement by Fidelity of a new online service for private users: Investor's Express. Born in the 1930s, the Fidelity group of Boston became the first discount broker in the United States after the liberalization of 1975 and has created numerous companies that offer financial services and products to individuals. Through Fidelity Brokerage Services it offers trading on the Trade*Plus platform, which however in April 1986 will be replaced by a proprietary system. In 1992 Investor's Express will become Fidelity On-line Xpress (FOX), adding a touch tone telephone to the PC. While offering, at least initially, the same platform as CD Anderson, Investor's Express has a very different fate and quickly becomes a success: in five months it becomes the first online trading service by diffusion in the United States and in March 1985 it will have already reached the 1,000 customers, preparing to become the online tool of many small and medium US local banks. The service initially offers only OTC stock and options and costs $195 to subscribe upon entry, plus a connection fee of 30 cents per hour in open markets and 10 cents per hour in closed markets and on weekends. Investor's Express then makes the Dow Jones News/Retrieval database available to customers by paying a one-off $12 plus $8 a month.

The bank's forecast is that 35% of customers will subscribe to the online service in three years. Between 1984 and 1985, Charles Schwab, who at that time was already one of the most important US intermediaries with nearly a million clients and $1.5 billion in managed capital, also took the field. Three years after having implemented the BETA (Brokerage Execution and Transaction Analysis) internal telematic system, it gives life to The Equalizer, a system that provides a large database of stock exchange information, the possibility of processing this information and a trading system. online with dial-up connection, which is done on normal telephone lines through a modem, by dialing a dedicated telephone number each time.

However, the service is not very successful, not only for the intrinsic slowness of the dial-up connection, but also because the screens are all text and without graphics (the operating system on which it is based is DOS), making the processing rather complex. The Equalizer will be replaced in 1993 by SmartStreet. In February 1985 the Hutton-line service (or Hutton line or The Hutton line) of the broker EF

Hutton & Co. is also active, which unlike Spear is part of the intermediary category who do not go through online services such as CompuServe but who are accessible through direct lines. In addition to trading, it offers information, news and data in real time, portfolio and account management, own studies and research and e-mail. Hutton's history is turbulent and, as in the case of North American Investments, there will be the intervention of more than one federal judge who will accelerate its closure, which took place formally in 1988. Born in 1904 in California, its name refers to the founder, Edward Francis Hutton, legendary for his ability to silence everyone the moment he starts talking: "When EF Hutton talks, people listen ("When he talks, people listen") is a very common way of saying US financials also currently; an example is the recent joke about US President Barack Obama by a TV commentator, who called him "the anti-EF Hutton" for his lack of charisma. In the 1970s and 1980s, the group founded by Edward Francis became an important financial player headed by a bank and numerous service companies, active in every financial sector.

In 1981, however, the troubles began that led to the merger with a company of American Express, that is, to the closure. What happened? In 1970 Robert Fomon became chief executive officer. From 1972, the year it was listed on the stock exchange, to 1982, the growth of the group appears unstoppable, thanks above all to the rapid reaction to the liberalization of financial intermediation which took place in 1975: Hutton opens branches throughout the country, has about 4,000 executives and declares revenues for about $1.1 billion, more than Merrill Lynch, for example, is able to do, while Fomon's right-hand man George Ball starts the private client services business. However, competition is strong and in the face of slowing revenues, the costs of the retail area (the activities towards individuals) take off progressively until they are out of control. Disorganization and improvisation in business decisions, later confirmed by most of the management, aggravate the situation.

In 1982, with the release of Ball, the retail area was entrusted to an executive with no experience in the sector and who, moreover, a few weeks later suffered a serious accident that forced him to stay away from the office for a long time. In this precarious situation, the online trading service for individuals is launched. In 1984 the first bomb explodes: a Pennsylvania district attorney opens a court case against Hutton for carrying out a scam in the form of check kiting: the company would have issued checks for an amount greater than the available balance on the accounts opened at several banks. using each other as a guarantee for the other in order to overcome inventory checks. In this way, in the "empty" periods between the issuance of checks and the control, the huge funds obtained are not burdened with any interest. Basically, Hutton would have borrowed at no cost at the expense of the other banks.

The investigation will ascertain that the illegal practices began in 1980. In the summer of 1985, Fomon agrees to plead the company guilty before a judge, which is sentenced to pay a fine of ten million dollars, a fine all in all.

Fomon resigns. In 1986 the company was in sharp decline due to the escape of customers, but fate was adverse and two more knock-out hits awaited it within a week of each other: an internal investigation revealed that the Providence branch was transformed into a money laundering center from a family of Cosa Nostra, the American mafia; the fact was immediately reported to the SEC and federal investigations started, with strong repercussions on the already blurred image of the group. A few days later, October 19, is the fateful "Black Monday" of the world stock exchanges and the collapse is sudden and doubledigit. Surrender arrives in November: the EF Hutton & Co. group is taken over by Shearson (American Express group) and Lehman Brothers and is renamed Shearson Lehman Hutton.

In addition to representing one of the first examples of "supernova" in the online trading sector, in the sense of a phenomenon that explodes brightly but disappears just as quickly, leaving only dust, the Hutton story also gives us the opportunity for another reflection. And that is that online trading is indeed experienced in its early stages by pioneers and innovative entrepreneurs, but in reality, it represents, for those who offer it, a tool among others to take advantage of a moment of chaotic and fulminating growth of a sector just liberalized. The dates speak for themselves: in 1975 the commission monopoly held by the NYSE was suppressed, in the period 1975-1981 there was a boom in discount brokers (from zero to 4,000 in five years). But the latter are not, like traditional brokers, oriented towards a clientele of companies and the rich, rather, precisely because of the prices charged, they have as their natural target the average American, the small and medium bourgeoisie, the middle class. A huge pool from which to draw capital to manage and on which to profit. A pool, however, which is interested not only by "discount brokers" but obviously also by small, medium, and large banks, which now run the risk of having substantial shares stolen. Competition is therefore "horizontal" (between discount brokers) but also "vertical" (between financial companies and banks that are very different from each other in terms of size, financial resources and products offered). And the United States, in the stereotype widespread in Europe, is the land where unscrupulousness and opportunity go hand in hand.

Competition is rampant, trading fees drop dramatically (as will happen in all countries where online trading will be introduced later) but overhead costs remain stable. So how to reduce the latter even more to make ends meet? The solution is new technologies, microcomputers (ancestors of current computers), computer networks, which are slow, not very homogeneous, and fragmented but already widespread, and their connection to the stock exchanges.

As in other sectors, even online trading for finance is ultimately nothing more than a new channel of contact with new customers, which allows you to reduce overhead costs and continue earning on intermediation, perhaps adding other services gradually, such as financial databases or stock market news. Without forgetting that almost all the pioneers of trading have a long tradition of traditional financial intermediation and consultancy behind them, made up of clients received in the office who are made available to experts able to assess their needs, manage their portfolio, recommend products. of other affiliated companies and so on. And this tradition will almost never be put aside, rather it will continue in parallel with the development of technological services. Only with the second generation of telematic brokers, which arose from the 1990s on the basis of previous experiences, will the first completely online intermediaries appear, without branches or consultants or promoters. These will then be able to fully boast the "title" of online broker. It should also be emphasized that the birth of online trading is disconnected, if not in direct opposition, from home banking; the management of current accounts and banking services is in fact offered by different companies to different customers with respect to online trading and only after many years will banks begin to integrate telematic trading of financial securities into home banking. A trend that has recently started and is giving very different and contradictory results.

A sign that online finance, a young business, on a global level has not yet found its true balance. However, if on the supply side there is nothing other than the need (or the desire) to squeeze everything possible out of the new competitive situation, it must be said that customers will also have a lot to gain from this chaos of technological-financial innovations. and not only in terms of costs: speed of access, decision-making autonomy, independence in the management of one's assets are essential pluses for a large slice of investors, who will nevertheless remain a niche to this day. With the spread of telematic finance at the level of stock exchanges and financial intermediaries, the SEC must also intervene to regulate the sector: on 9 October 1984 it issued the "Notice of Commission views on computer brokerage system" number 34-21383, which, when the Internet was still it is not accessible to the general public and the Web would not have been born before ten years, it lays the foundations for ad hoc regulation of telematic intermediaries, starting with the authorization requirement and a specific register for them separate from traditional "broker dealers". It is, the legal sources of the time note, "apparently the first citation by the SEC of brokerage systems via computer", which rather than dictating precise rules of conduct takes care to underline that those who combine online trading systems with automatic systems for sending stock exchange signals, buy or sell recommendations, or trading advice in any form, including as "urgent recommendations". As you can easily guess, this is a very heartfelt issue in those years, especially because, as mentioned, the discount brokers mostly turned to generally inexperienced customers and therefore, according to the adversaries of automated trading, potentially able to be manipulated with ease.

The "Black Monday" of 1987
Online trading stops

The nascent telematic financial industry, however, suffered a severe blow on October 19, 1987, with the "Black Monday": world markets collapsed by 20%, 30%, 40% and even 60% (that of New Zealand, for which we speak, however, of "Black Tuesday" due to the time zone) in a single session. The blame is placed on the so-called "program trading", a type of negotiation of groups of securities which, linked to the increased ability of computer systems to process a large number of orders in a very short time, would have favored massive and uncontrolled sales. An important part of the responsibility is in fact attributed to the automatic trading systems adopted by banks and investment funds, programmed to sell if certain thresholds in the prices of the securities or the values of the indices are breached. However, not everyone shares the thesis of program trading, preferring to impeach a speculative bubble, the scarce liquidity of the market or referring to the psychology of the markets.
The Brady Commission, commissioned by the US Parliament to investigate the causes of the event, concluded that the collapse had originated from complex credit strategies of large institutional investors known as index

arbitrage and portfolio insurance. Sales start solid on the Hong Kong stock exchange, which sees its index plummeting 45.5% after a very bad week on the NYSE, and quickly spread to Europe and the United States, areas where the lists have not yet introduced. mechanisms for suspension of trading in the event of an excess of downside, which will happen precisely following the events of the "Black Monday". The Dow Jones index will leave 508 points on the ground, equal to almost 23% of its value. The Milan Stock Exchange index, on the other hand, will resist much better than others: the drop is contained by -10.84%, but it will be followed by an "even more black Tuesday" at -12.22%.

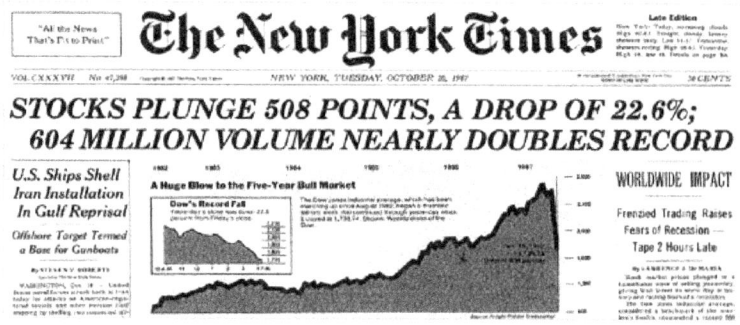

Figure 16 • The collapse of the "Black Monday" markets (October 19, 1987) on the front page of the "New York Times"

According to a study by Amen & Associates (and never a company name was more suitable for such an occasion), compared to the data of January 1987, 786 of the largest fund managers in the United States have lost on average 40% of capital in management, amounting to approximately $500 billion. The situation is dramatic for many savers, aggravated by the fact that in the moment of collapse and panic few managed to contact their brokers, stormed through every available channel, PC, telephone, office, fax, to close orders. and get rid of the titles that fall precipitously. According to Joseph Meth of DailyMarkets.com, "Some investors lost millions of dollars instantly, while other unstable individuals who were also engulfed in the crash went to their broker's offices and started shooting; many brokers were killed, even though they had no control over what was happening on the market».

Another effect of "Black Monday" is the boom in hostile takeovers. Indeed, with prices collapsing, many previously inaccessible companies become attractive even to those who do not have immense fortunes; for this reason, the large corporations immediately throw themselves into the purchase of their shares with the aim of preventing actions of this type, while those who no longer have the money to react, suffer. Much like jackals roaming between the corpses of a battle, European, Japanese, and Australian companies between late 1987 and early 1988 shop hands down, spending $15.5 billion on non-stop takeovers. friendly, while in the first three months of 1988, according to Merge & Acquisition magazine, the overall outlay for the acquisition of US companies at clearing prices is at least 80 billion dollars, which by the end of 1988 will have become at least 180 billion.

A few weeks later, at the end of a conference, about thirty analysts and economists from all over the world will predict endless catastrophes starting from the "Black Monday" and mindful of the
1929 crisis. However, it will quickly be denied by events: after 19 October, in fact, the markets will inexorably begin to recover the lost ground. Before returning to normal,

however, the online broker sector and finance in general will take a few years. The event is a real flush, which sweeps away hundreds of financial companies (300 in the United States alone, out of 12,000 active), puts thousands in crisis and completely transforms the faces of others: not just customers, for fear or for having lost everything, they stop trading both traditionally and electronically severely slowing down the flow of commissions they generate, but also the securities portfolios of the financial companies themselves evaporate. Por example, the aforementioned Hutton in a single day loses $78 million and Charles Schwab $22 million, with the latter's number of trades going from 16,000 per day to less than 10,000 in the following weeks and commission revenues plummeting. by 40%, closing the nine months of the year with profits down by 80% compared to the same period of the previous year (6.7 million against 33 million).

"The trading volume is contracting we read on the E*Trade website page relating to those events and the online trading services, including Trade*Plus, are withering away". Por the next three years online trading will be put in mothballs, and you will hardly hear about new initiatives. Worsening the situation is finally the wave of scandals and arrests that hit many US financial companies and listed companies, a storm that at the end of the 1980s concretized the investigations of the SEC and the FBI in sensational arrests of executives, searches, trials and very high fines for insider trading, price manipulation and investor scams.

Among the best-known names involved in the scandals of those years, Dennis Levine, Ivan Boesky and Michael Milken, expert in mergers and acquisitions the first, trader the second, influential expert in junk bond the third. The investigations on them (since 1986 also carried out by the future mayor of New York Rudolph Giuliani, among others) uncover a vast network of collusion and complicity in financial circles that lead to dozens of trials and convictions: three years in prison and 100 million a fine to Boesky, four years and $362,000 to Levine, compensation of $1.1 billion and a ten-year sentence (later reduced to two) for Milken.

The scandals of the late 1980s contributed to greatly damaging the image of finance among the public of savers and investors, who since then have identified the sector as a sea populated by sharks waiting for defenseless minnows. The only lighthouse in the night will be PC Financial Networks (or PC Financial or PCFN), an online trading service for individuals born in 1988 from a collaboration between the financial group Donaldson Lufkin & Jenrette (DLJ) and the clearing house Pershing & Co., in short. also acquired by DLJ. However, if someone does not know whether to consider PCFN the latest innovation of the first phase or the first of the new era, we can immediately remove all doubts: chronologically it is obviously a post-"Black Monday" online broker, but in reality it was born from a project started in the previous years and is the child of pre-collapse euphoria.

The only difference is that, having arrived on the market a few months after "Black Monday", it will at least manage to survive instead of plunging into the abyss of the crisis. At least up to what for the USA represents the period of the real boom in online trading, i.e., the two-year period 1996-97.

In fact, in the first years of its life, PCFN recorded very limited growth, both due to the difficult general economic-financial situation, and due to some initial marketing choices, that turned out to be unfortunate. Until 1996, users did not exceed 10,000 units, with an average growth of only 1,250 customers per year, and only from this date, thanks to the agreement with the online service Prodigy, the company's online business will take off. In the 90s PCFN will in fact become one of E*Trade most fierce commercial rivals. DLJ will dominate Prodigy while E*Trade will dictate the law on CompuServe and the two big rivals will then divide America On Line users practically equally. However, the advent of the Web will change the rules of the game. Founded in 1959 by William Donaldson and Dan Lufkin, the DLJ group will be acquired by Credit Suisse in 2001. PCFN will change its name in 1997 and become DLJ Direct, to become CSFB-Direct since 2001; sold by the Swiss group to Bank of Montreal in 2002, it was finally taken over by E*Trade in 2006. After ten years of commercial battles and five years of decline due to the situation of the parent group (but also to the simultaneous decline of Prodigy crushed by competition) the group founded by Porter therefore triumphs on the field against the archenemy. And PCFN will be just one of several "victims" of the E*Trade steamroller, which throughout its history will absorb numerous smaller online brokers, including Web Street Securities, Harrisdirect and BrownCo. In the 1990s, the commissions charged by PCFN were $40 for orders over $2,500 and $100 plus 0.1% for orders starting at $40,000 in value.

CHAPTER 3

The 90s and the second generation of online brokers

The period from 1990 to 1994 represents for the USA a phase of relaunch, both for the economy, the stock exchange and finance in general, and for online trading. And at the end of this phase, we will find the birth of the World Wide Web, the first disruptive European trading services (which did not experience the pioneering phase of the 1980s) and, on the US market, 12 online brokers including the large US players who before the recent subprime crisis they seemed to be the dominating granite of the decade.
The recovery then lends a hand to the development of services and technology, stimulating new businesses and new ideas, but above all by drastically reducing the costs of the technological tools necessary for trading (PCs, networks, software) and spreading others widely (modems),

creating thus the conditions for the subsequent mass phenomena linked to social networks and the sharing of digital resources.

In those first days of rebirth, E*Trade represents the pure and successful online broker par excellence, while the others will follow in his footsteps not without effort and not without changing business model over the following years. In fact, it will be common to see brokers who, in the face of poor trading successes, will support online investment and savings management services and will turn into a bank to offer current accounts, credit cards, loans, mortgages and so on, often opening physical branches and integrating ever more numerous networks of promoters.

Models that combine the components mentioned in different ways and times, in search of a balance between profitability and quality of service, between the need for huge investments in IT structures and commissions with increasingly reduced revenues due to the low barriers to entry and of the increasingly fierce competition. Models that from the initial dualism between specialized intermediaries (online brokers focused on online trading) and "all-in-one" intermediaries (the latter mostly banks that integrate an online trading service with the rest of their more or less rich offer of traditional banking products) will evolve in different directions.

1990-1994 Brokers of pre-WWW era recovery

Returning to the years of recovery, some online services already active continue their growth, such as those of Charles Schwab (directly or through the Genie online service) and Fidelity (also direct or through Dow Jones News I Retrieval), which in July 1993, for example, offer a 10% discount on brokerage fees to anyone who trades via computer or tone phone. Schwab also replaced the outdated The Equalizer system with StreetSmart in 1993.
On CompuServe the activity of Quick & Reilly continues, on Prodigy the presence of PCFN is still a constant. Schwab, Fidelity, and Quick & Reilly were defined by the press of the time as "the big three": they are in fact the largest brokers on the market, full-service brokers, and non-discount brokers, obviously also considering the predominant traditional activities carried out in the branch and not online. "Kiplinger's Magazine" of July 1994 lists eight US online brokers: Charles Schwab with the StreetSmart service, Fidelity Investment with Fidelity On-line Xpress (FOX), Accutrade (these first three indicated as direct connection brokers, i.e., without the need to use online services for trading with them), DLJ with PCFN, E*Trade, Quick & Reilly with QuickWay online Brokerage Services, Max Ule with Tickerscreen and Trade*Plus. And of these, only E*Trade is a pure online intermediary, i.e., without physical branches.
According to research carried out in 2001 by the American Association of Individual Investors (AAII), in 1991 only 6 online brokers would be active in the USA, all obviously in

direct connection and on non-Internet networks; three years later, in 1994, there are 7 and in 1995 they become 12, of which one (Wall Street Investor Services or perhaps K. Aufhauser & Co.) first ever to be landed on the Web. With some difference between the Kiplinger's data and those of the AAII (a difference of a few months between 1994 and 1995 due to a different vision of the starting point of the companies, i.e., the date of foundation rather than the date of the actual launch of the trading service) the numbers confirm that in the sector, as niche as it will always be, something is happening. In recent years, therefore, the number of online intermediaries is still limited to very few experimenters, so much so as to even write in numerous American texts of the time that in 1994 there was no account for online intermediation in the USA and that instead "in 1999 there were 5 million active".

An untrue statement, the first, and reductive the second, given that if Tom Tisch, vice president of Trade*Plus, estimated in July 1994 that there are at least 100,000 US investors who trade financial securities via pc (not to mention that trading has already been offered in the United States for over ten years) and if Forrester Research estimates for 1999 about 8.4 million online trading accounts in the United States alone; number, among other things, which gives the idea of the explosion of online trading that will take place in a few years.

An explosion that, given the pre-"Black Monday" experience, no one expects, instead estimating a significant, slow and constant but not amazing growth.

In fact, no one imagines that shortly thereafter, at the large laboratory of the European Council for Nuclear Research (CERN), in the heart of the European continent a few kilometers from Geneva, in addition to the theoretical reconstruction of the physical universe, work is being carried out on the construction of a new virtual universe: the World Wide Web. Nor can anyone imagine that the creation of the British Tim Berners-Lee and the Belgian Robert Cailliau will also give a tremendous boost to online trading. In any case, the US experience has already produced its first effects also beyond the Atlantic, both at the level of markets and advanced financial instruments and of network technologies. The aforementioned European experiences of Videotex and SWIFT, to do but two examples among many, are only the light of the beginning of a phenomenon which has not yet stopped, and which reserves surprises at every step. The development of networks and digital data processing is unstoppable even in the Old Continent and progressively pervades all sectors, civil and military, albeit with more limited resources than those in the United States, with legislation and industrial policies that are decidedly less favorable to the development of innovative companies and with strong control on the part of governments and public bodies.

As far as we are concerned, however, the electronic trading of securities appears in Europe only in 1994, that is 12 years after the launch of Tickerscreen by Max Ule & Co., also under the impetus of the recovery of the financial markets. And it is for this reason that, except for a quick reference to the subsequent developments on the western shore of the Atlantic, in the next volumes we will abandon the history of North American trading to focus on the European one and therefore on the Italian one.

The growth of online trading is also favored by the decrease in commissions requested from customers. Just take a look at the average commission per executed: from the liberalization of discount brokers in 1975 to 1994 it remains around 45 dollars (traditional intermediaries apply rates up to ten times higher), while in the next three years it will drop by 10 dollars (-22 % approximately), and then start to fall again in 1997 to $20 (-55%), a level at which it will then remain for the following years. It is no coincidence that 1997 is considered the boom year of online trading in the USA, therefore also the year of the start of the ruthless competition favored by the WWW. However, what characterizes these years of transition from the financial crisis to the Web is above all the birth of some companies focused on online trading which in a very short time will act as bridges towards the new technological era, that of the World Wide Web and the "single world network. ".

In fact, these are realities that are not born with platforms developed expressly for the Web and for its amazing "hypertextual language", but which in a few months will be able to grasp first of all the new technological wave and throw themselves headlong into it. And since these are names that have almost completely disappeared from memory, many may wonder what happened to these pioneers. The answer is simple: they were all bought by the big players born and raised before "Black Monday" and survived the big flush, which will make them the backbone of their next online business.

The protagonists of this second pioneering wave are Wall Street Investor Services (born in 1993 and became Wall Street Access in 1996, in 2004 it sold its online activities towards retail to E*Trade) and K. Aufhauser & Co. (1994, absorbed in 1995) by Ameritrade), to which must be added National Discount Brokers (January 1994, October 2000 at Deutsche Bank), Jack White & Co. (1973, acquired by Ameritrade in March 1997) and Net Investors (division of HoweBarnes founded in 1994; the entire group was acquired by Raymond James in 2011); however, the latter three all make use, at least for the first few years, of the PAWWS service provided by Securities APL.

To these we can then add Waterhouse Securities (later Waterhouse National Bank), which in

1992 started the trading service via touch-phone on the US west coast and which in the same year began to develop a real online trading service. will see the light only four years later. This second generation of online brokers, however, while representing a "bridge" phenomenon between the past and the future, is more closely linked to what will be the third brood, that is to what we could fully define the "Web generation". However, carefully underlining the difference, mentioned above, between the Internet and the Web, of which the latter is only a part of the former characterized by graphics and hypertextuality, therefore by a great ease of understanding even for less experienced users. Features that will make the Web very commercially usable. Therefore, these intermediaries are the pioneers of a generational transition that will mark the future of online trading: we will deal with them in the next chapter.

But first let's look at what has been the real turning point of these years, destined to change the face of the market through a new business model.

In 1991, the founder of Trade*Plus William Porter, thanks to a loan from the company of which he is a partner of a few hundred thousand dollars, founded E*Trade Securities, which since 1992 has offered an online trading service through the networks of America On. Line and CompuServe; a fortune, given that these two great online services will dominate the market for years and that in 1994 they will have together about 8 million users, technological, wealthy, and interested in news. The perfect target for online trading services.

Compared to Trade*Plus which was sold "turnkey" to other companies the business model is that of a real discount broker, that is, a discount broker, which offers its service directly to private customers, with a fixed commission (flat, i.e., "flat" and not monthly or on consumption) at a strong discount compared to those practiced on the market and with free stock market data. Again, Porter rides the right horse. Although, he says, "being a financial intermediary is not a profession you would like to see your child do". It takes determination and a strong stomach, which he obviously does not lack.

Since 1992 the markets have taken off, technology has spread and E*Trade, which has become a bank, remains one of the big names in the US and world sector for the next fifteen years. With the stock market boom, Americans are returning to investing in publicly traded stocks and in

1995 about 20% of the US population owns shares, up from just 5% 10 years earlier. In 1992 the company closed the balance sheet with a turnover of 850,000 dollars, which at the end of '94 will have become 11 million with 355,455 open accounts and over 22 million in '95, with 2.6 million profits thanks to commissions for the execution of "only" $40, but also a high-quality, 24-hour online information service. The group reorganizes and what was previously only a bet by the founder becomes the main business and the engine of growth: the 44 employees in 1994 become

200 in 1995 and will continue to grow. In August 1996 E*Trade is listed on the stock exchange and the two historical founders retire: Newcomb gives life to a non-profit foundation, Porter gives way to another historical E*Trade executive, Christos Cotsakos. The strengths of

E*Trade are well outlined in the report made in November 1999 by two researchers from the Center for Research on Information Technology and Organizations of the University of California entitled "On-line brokerages: E*Trade vs. Charles Schwab", who compares the two business models in detail, which will soon become great rivals. The substantial difference is that Schwab was born as a traditional intermediary, then it becomes a discount broker with a strong technological footprint initially directed towards internal processes, later turning it towards customers; all this while maintaining its physical branches, which in 1999 will be 295 throughout the United States. In short, a traditional-online hybrid model capable of guaranteeing profitability even in times of crisis.

Conversely, E*Trade was born after the experience of Trade*Plus and as a pure online broker, that is, offering only the access channels of online services and direct connection, first, and then the Internet, in addition of course to the omnipresent telephone to device tones also with voice recognition.

E*Trade offers, in addition to actual online trading, the ability to monitor your investment portfolio, applications for the processing of graphs and stock market data, comments and market analysis in real time, news and information on listed companies (in particular, through the CNN Financial Network, the EDGAR database which collects all mandatory documents of listed companies and access to SEC documentation relating to placements), all 24 hours a day, seven days a week.

The instruments offered are shares, options and mutual funds (a category, the latter, which has long been widespread on telematic services), while the only market available is the NASDAQ, which is accompanied by a list of other shares and options. on indices and tradable funds on an internal E*Trade circuit.

Numerous types of orders are also available on the trading platform, including market, limit (valid until cancellation or until the end of the session) and stop, and it is possible to trade downwards (short), trade notifications are sent to the platform (many brokers still send notifications via email or regular mail) and clients then receive their business details at home in the form of a paper letter.

There are numerous indications on the market trend, such as the best and worst stocks or the most active stocks of the day, and it is possible to set alarms on price levels or volatility of individual stocks. E*Trade also offers an automated system for the analysis and management of your portfolio capable of calculating profits and losses in real time at current prices and able to consider any special operations such as the detachment of dividends.

In the following years, E*Trade will also focus on the Web, while maintaining for a long time the agreements with America On Line, Prodigy, CompuServe, AT&T WorldNet and Microsoft Network, and entering into agreements with Yahoo, Banc One, Reuters News, Morningstar and many other companies. providers of financial services and content.

The model appears innovative and very aggressive, so as to make the company one of the first in the sector in a very short time. However, compared to competitors of much greater depth and perhaps with a less rapid approach in the integration of technological channels but more elastic and "hybrid" like Charles Schwab, it is the latter, as we shall see, that will give the best results in terms of economic growth. financial and solidity. The example of E*Trade, however, serves to shake up the market: the constant flow of technological development does not allow us to stand still and enjoy the positions conquered, because it takes very little to take the field with new initiatives and take away dozens of thousands of customers with new solutions, a good organization and above all a sophisticated and complete online offer of products, services, teaching, assistance and constantly decreasing commissions. From now on, those who want to try their hand successfully in the online trading arena will have to have huge capital behind them, clear ideas, and a strong orientation towards the constant implementation of technology and innovative solutions.

The pioneering phase ends here. And it is no coincidence that in the same period, starting from

1994, the first specialized online brokers also appeared in Europe. In short, the atmosphere in the financial world of the post-"Black Monday" has changed. The economy and finance have started to pull again, and the imminence of big news is in the air. It is no coincidence that on June 15, 1993, twelve large US financial intermediaries announced the creation of a new circuit for telematic trading, Intermarket Trading Network (ITN), a sort of private electronic exchange designed to connect exchanges, brokers and managers, pension and investment funds and other institutional investors quickly, efficiently and economically. Promoters of the initiative, based on the Merrin Financial platform, are Merrill Lynch, Salomon Brothers, Morgan Stanley, PaineWebber Incorporated, Execution Services, Investment Technology Group, Troster Singer, Capital Institutional Services, Arizona Stock Exchange (AZX) and Robinson Humphrey (Primerica/Smith Barney/Shearson group), but also two names already known to us: Herzog,

Heine & Geduld (that of Max Ule & Co.) and Fidelity Investments.

The World Wide Web

In the same year of the foundation of Trade*Plus, 1991, the European Council for Nuclear Research (CERN) in Geneva announces the existence of the World Wide Web (i.e., "world web", more simply "WWW" or "Web").
The CERN project was born in 1989 with the name of "Enquire" and was initially developed for internal use. Led by the English Tim Barners-Lee (considered the father of the Web) and the Belgian Robert Cailliau, from the first minute of existence the Web is characterized by a strong transnational imprint: CERN, in fact, consists of a large area not far away from Geneva occupied by dozens of buildings built right on the border between Switzerland and France. And the two buildings between which the first contact between a WWW server and a browser is made, building 31 (where the Web was developed) and building 2, are one in French territory and one in Swiss territory, albeit separated by a few tens of meters.

Figure 17 • The plaque at CERN in Geneva commemorating the birth of the World Wide Web

But why is the WWW the first step in a revolution? It is a hypertext system complete with a programming language (HTML) and an ad hoc transmission protocol (HTTP); hypertexts are texts on which specific parts can be highlighted through links which, once selected ("clicked"), allow access to further documents. This allows you to create documents (located on servers, i.e., accessible by multiple users at the same time) consisting of a very high number of pages, from each of which it is possible to pass to others in a non-sequential way, going back and changing the reading path depending on the need. An intuition that in a short time will give life to a virtual world made up of interactive documents, sites to "navigate" and pages to read and browse with what will be the first graphic "browser", Mosaic.
Here you can see the first website ever made:
http://www.w3.org/History/19921103hypertext/hypertext/WWW/TheProject.html
Mosaic, born in 1993 and on the basis of which almost all the browsers currently in circulation have been developed, was created by Marc Andreessen of the National Center for Supercomputing Applications (NCSA) at the University of

Illinois thanks to funds raised on the initiative of the then US Senator Al Gore. In 1994 Andreessen will set up on his own to develop the Mosaic project commercially and will call the company Netscape.

Starting in 1993, by decision of CERN, the WWW will become open and free, and will spread with such rapidity that today most users consider the terms WWW and Internet to be equivalent. Suffice it to say that in 1991 there were five sites, in 1992 no more than a dozen and in 1993 just over 600. But already at the end of 1994, the true year of the WWW boom, there are over 10,000, and it is from this date that the first commercial websites arise, some of which will be very successful. These include the first e-commerce site with an electronic payment system, First Virtual, the search engines Lycos and Yahoo!, the site of the magazine "Wired" and that of Pizza Hut, as well as the home page of the president of United States on Whitehouse.gov.

The most reliable estimate of the current number of Web sites, more than twenty years after the birth of the WWW, is about 580 million, which compared to 230-250 million in 2009 indicates that in the last three years there would have been an increase of well over 100%; a fact that must therefore be integrated with the consideration that about 70% of the sites are not active or not complete, not to mention that in recent years the fashion for blogs has exploded. Whatever the exact number, these are measurable quantities in the hundreds of millions. What matters to us is that 1994 is the year of the turning point: for financial intermediaries who turn to private individuals online, it no longer means investing in the dark, having to choose between a speck of protocols, networks, online services, software, and hardware based on many different standards and therefore unable to develop a sufficient critical mass of users. Now one Internet access channel takes over the others thanks to a set of intelligent technical solutions but also to the (relative) ease of use of the software that users have to use, which in turn force commercial offers to remain simple and graphically appealing. In short, a niche commercial channel is quickly starting to become mass, and all economic sectors are thrown headlong into it.

In the case of online trading, we have already mentioned the pioneers of the third generation: Wall Street Investor Services, K. Aufhauser & Co. and Securities APL (National Discount Brokers, Jack White & Co. and Net Investors are based on the latter). However, it should not be forgotten that 1994 is also the year in which the first Italian and European online brokers are born.

In chronological order it would seem that the first online broker via the Internet is Wall Street Access (WSA), founded in 1981 by Denis P. Kelleher. Arriving in the US from Ireland in 1958, Kelleher began his career as a delivery boy at Merrill Lynch; in 1976 he founded a first broker and in 1981 the company he still leads, in the form of a clearing house, gradually transforming it into a full-fledged intermediary.

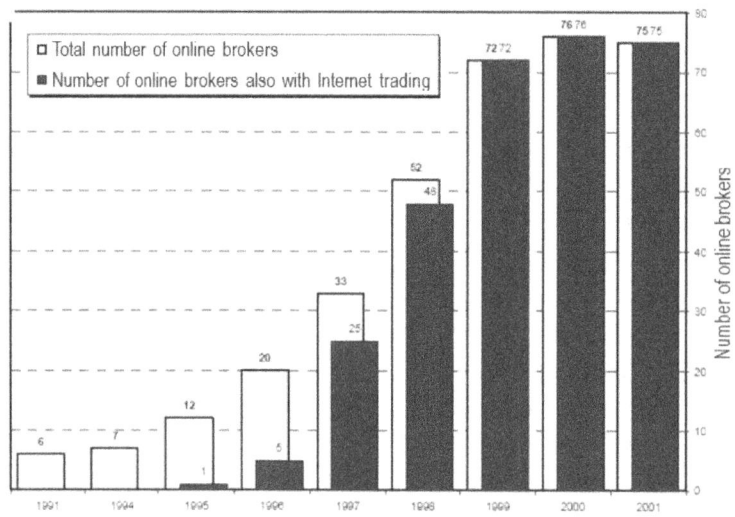

Figure 18 • Ratio between the number of overall online brokers and brokers who also o-er Internet Trading

1995-1996
The first modern online brokers

Among the prestigious positions that Kelleher has collected over the decades are the presidency of St. John's University and the Metropolitan Museum of Art, and the direction of the Staten Island Foundation. This latter position derives from the fact that he is very active in supporting immigrants from his country of origin, with whom he maintains a very close relationship, so much so that he also becomes economic adviser to the Irish prime minister.

The online trading service for private users, WSA online, was launched in 1993, but only between 1994 and 1995 will it land on the WWW based on Microsoft's software solutions (remember that Microsoft's operating system was born in 1985 and that in 1993 Windows NT was launched). He carves out a little space in history for having launched, the first ever, an online system for managing complex strategies with options. The company, which is still active, sold WSA online to E*Trade in 2004.

Then, in March 1995, the "Los Angeles Times" consecrated Wall Street Access as "the first on-line trading system over the World Wide Web". The service offers trading in shares and options with real-time quotes through a web platform (i.e., not on a specific client but by connecting to the site), into which mutual funds and bonds will later be integrated. In a few years, the commission per execution on the shares will drop to around $20, $50 for funds and $1.35 with a minimum of $19.50 for options contracts. The required margin is 2.652% and they can also open accounts with WSAs residing abroad. Initially, the broker offers an application for managing its securities portfolio, Stock Trader, for $59.95 and will sell approximately 30,000 copies. Subsequently, it will make it available for free to users as a lever to attract new customers. WSA online is considered a service for heavy traders. In 1994 the moment to relaunch the management of stock exchange orders via the Internet for private clients finally appears ripe for Keith R. Aufhauser, an American descendant of a family of Munich bankers, who transforms the New York broker he founded in 1981 (K. Aufhauser & Co.) in what contends with Wall Street Access for the title of first intermediary via the Internet for private traders in history.

At first, however, it relies on non-Web online services which, unlike for example CompuServe used by Trade*Plus, allow lump-sum and not hourly billing of connection costs; this therefore allows you to always carry out your business online without being forced to work offline to connect only when the order is sent, under penalty of exorbitant costs. However, this approach only lasts a few months, given that already towards the end of 1994 Aufhauser launches a trading service through the WealthWeb platform, which saw its first test order in August 1994. In 1995 Aufhauser's commission for execution it is 34 dollars for the first 1,700 shares traded, then 2 cents for each subsequent share: a little less than what Charles Schwab practiced, when those of the large traditional intermediaries fluctuate between 100 and 300 dollars. Quotes are delayed by 15-20 minutes. Shortly thereafter, Aufhauser introduces a special account for $800 a year all-inclusive and for $30 a month stock prices in (almost) real time. In 1995, sensing the deal, the financial group Ameritrade took over K. Aufhauser & Co. from the founder, entering a competition for the conquest of the new telematic market that is becoming increasingly bitter across the Atlantic. Today Keith Aufhauser heads up Aufhauser Securities in New York.

Also in 1995, Securities APL launched the Portfolio Accounting World Wide Service (PAWWS). Led by president and CEO Jay Whipple, the company is a kind of evolved Trade*Plus, in the sense that, like Porter's creature, it does not work directly with private clients but offers its outsourced services to banks, intermediaries, institutional investors. and managers; among these services, all based on complex hardware and software infrastructures, there is the "turnkey" supply of online tools for managing customer portfolios, for measuring financial performance, for executing orders on the stock exchange and to create advanced reporting systems, precisely through the PAWWS platform. In May 1996, shortly before being acquired by Checkfree Corp. through a stock exchange for the equivalent of approximately $53 million, Securities APL has as clients the top 180 Wall Street financial firms, on whose behalf it manages electronically about 300,000 professional portfolios and hundreds of thousands of executed orders per day. And his clients include online brokers Jack White, National Discount Brokers and Net Investor.

Founded in 1973, California-based Jack White & Co started an online trading service in 1995; it is a simple service, accessible from a website and not well suited to the impetuous growth in demand that White must face in those months (10,000 customers in 1998), as well as being focused almost only on customers in the San Diego area. Within a couple of years, White will also completely restructure its infrastructure and will abandon PAWWS to build an online trading service entirely based on Microsoft architecture and applications. One of the services most used by users is the Mutual Fund Network, or the possibility of subscribing about 6,600 online funds, of which
1,250 without subscription fees. Broadly speaking, therefore, White's offer is comparable to that of Schwab, that is, strongly focused on investment and savings products for feuding users (and on collateral services such as credit cards), but with a service of trading that for three years in a row, from '94 to '96, was awarded by the magazine "Smart Money", the magazine of the "Wall Street Journal", as the

best in the United States. In March 1998 Jack White & Co. was acquired by the Canadian Toronto-Dominion Bank for 100 million dollars; TD Bank already incorporated Waterhouse Investor Services for 714 million in 1996, creating the subsidiary TD Waterhouse, which in 2006 will finally be acquired by Ameritrade giving life to TD Ameritrade.

In this regard, it is worth dwelling on Ameritrade's takeover of the North American online trading market, which with the merger with TD Waterhouse becomes one of the top four or five world giants in the sector. As we have already seen when discussing services via touch-tone telephone, its story begins in Omaha, Nebraska, with the name of Firts Omaha Securities, which will change first to Accutrade, then to TransTerra and from 1996 to Ameritrade; its acquisitions campaign develops through

K. Aufhauser & Co. and All American Brokers (1995) which since 1996 have been integrated into the online trading service "Accutrade for Windows" and then into eBroker; in 1999 the RJ Forbes group was taken over, in 2001 TradeCast and National Discount Brokers, in 2002 Datek online, in 2003 Mydiscountbroker.com, in 2004 Bidwell, Brokerage America, Investex and JB Oxford, and in 2006 precisely TD Waterhouse. With E*Trade, Charles Schwab and Fidelity, TD Ameritrade thus becomes one of the main players in the sector worldwide.

In the same year of her marriage to Ameritrade, TD Waterhouse launches Waterhouse Investors PC Network, which offers clients online trading, direct access to financial markets, real-time pricing, market news and account management. The growth of TD Ameritrade is paradigmatic of the path of all the major players in international online trading, developed on the basis of traditional intermediation of the previous decades and then enlarged thanks to the acquisition of a dust of pioneering and innovative small and medium-sized companies.

Going back to the brokers linked to the PAWWS of Securities APL, another important name is undoubtedly National Discount Brokers. The company was founded in 1994 as a traditional discount broker within the Sherwood financial group (struggling to recover from a series of setbacks during the 1980s). Not, therefore, online and with a strong orientation to telephone trading, so as to ensure a maximum response to the third ring in advertising: otherwise, the execution of the order is free. In October 1994, NDB presented the online trading service via the Web through the PAWWS, to which in 1996 an extensive mutual fund trading service was added. In 1997 the whole group will be renamed NDB and in October 2000 it will be taken over by Deutsche Bank, when it will register approximately 270,000 customers. As with other APL Securities brokers, NDB also offers WWW trading on stocks, bonds, mutual funds, and options, as well as financial information, real-time pricing, portfolio management, stock exchange data processing tools and stock selection. The commissions, defined by the media of the time as "the most aggressive compared to other online brokers", were 20 dollars for executed on OTC shares or 28 dollars for orders of at least 5,000 listed shares.

Lastly, the service called "Net Investors" created by the intermediary Howe Barnes in December
1994 and fully operational in 1995 is less competitive: up to $38 for orders over $2,500 in value, with confirmation of the execution via email. However, the two-year period '95 - '96 is a nursery of online brokers.

Thomas F. White & Co. proves to be one of the most active companies in the sector with three online brokers under its control: Lombard Institutional Brokerage, CompuTEL Securities and White Discount Securities.

In October 1995 Lombard Institutional Brokerage entered the market with a competitive online trading offer, starting with a website for trading options; the commission per execution is 34 dollars, both via the Internet and via telephone-voice and provides customers, among other things, with advanced graphs and indications for investments (it is still a traditional intermediary that bases its business on counseling). The platform is developed internally and shortly after Lombard will come to the spin-off of the development activity to sell its technology to other brokers. CompuTEL Securities and White Discount Securities both offer the same service, called the "Rapid Trade System", which allows trading both via computer and via touch-tone telephone. CompuTEL has been in business since June 1995 and offers trading on stocks, options, funds, and bonds.

The history and the end of TF White & Co. are closely linked to a legal matter in which its founder Thomas White was involved starting in February 2003. Four months from this date the company changed its name to Acument Securities, and then definitively close its doors shortly after. Also, in these years Pacific Brokerage Services (PBS), founded in 1976 by Steve Wallace in Los Angeles, took the field. Historical and large discount broker, in 1995 presented its online trading service, initially with dial-up connection (i.e., direct via modem and telephone cable) and three years later via the Internet on the basis of an IBM AS I 400 server and I I Net software. Shortly after, however, it was taken over by Mellon Bank, merged with the traditional broker

Dreyfus Brokerage Services (founded in 1976), which has been offering online trading in stocks and options since 1996. In 2001 it was integrated, with its 75,000 active accounts, into Brown & Co., Which was then sold to E*Trade. The roundup of the two-year period '95 -'96 continues with another important actor on the US scene, Datek, involved in more than one financial scandal but firmly present in the first places of all the rankings of online brokers, for quality and size, of the following years.

To launch it are Sheldon Maschler and Robert E. Brennan, the first shock trader in New York, the second seller of penny stocks (shares of very small companies, often listed on OTC circuits, whose prices can be easily manipulated by financial organizations without scruples). But Maschler took his first steps, starting in 1989 at the age of 44, with two teenagers, the seventeen-year-old son of a friend, Jeffrey A. Citron, and the high school student and computer genius Joshua Levine; with them it develops the Watcher and Monster Key programs, able to monitor the exchanges on the NASDAQ system for trading on OTC securities called Small Order Execution System (SOES) and take advantage of its weaknesses. In 1988, however, the NASDAQ manager discovers the trick and imposes a $60,000 fine on him; in 1991, when Citron and Maschler, however, already pocketed a total of 3 million dollars, Datek was suspended from the SOES for 35 days for abuse of the system. And again, a suspension of three months in 1992 and another of one day in 1993, this time for "profane and indecent language". In 1992, Maschler's two partners left the company to found ECN Island. The fame of Datek and his managers is equal to that of a pirate ship attacking passing ships, so much so that the less offensive nickname that runs is "SOES bandit". In any case, suspensions and fines will be the constant in the activity of Maschler and former partners for a long time. Suffice it to say that again in January 2003 Maschler and Citron will be sentenced by the SEC to pay $30 and $22 million respectively for illegal trading and book manipulation. Other sanctions will come in 1997 and 1998.

Since 1996, the New York-based company has dedicated body and soul to online trading, once again basing its success on the ability to develop software with a high level of complexity. Also, because in the meantime the NASD announces stricter rules regarding the use of applications for institutional trading, which among other things are now used by many other companies.

However, Datek is able to exploit the full potential of Island, which offers many stocks listed on the NASDAQ often at cheaper prices, and this allows to start a price war against other brokers by bringing the commission per execution to the lowest levels never seen before: $9.99. In 1998, Datek registered 80,000 customers and ranks fifth in the US for average daily volume transacted. Finally, it was in 1996 that the maximum weight of traditional and online discount trading took place. Founded in 1963, Charles Schwab & Co. comes online relatively late compared to the competition, but its numbers (over 25 billion dollars managed) and the weight of its investments allow it not only to maintain but also to increase its share market. In 1995 he launched his first website and at the same time took over the British ShareLink; in 1996 he started online trading via the Web (eSchwab), after having invested in technology already in 1979 with the installation of the first servers for internal use, having launched The Eguilizer in 1983, in 1989 TeleBroker (automated telephone trading system) and in 1993 StreetSmart.

Compared to E*Trade, Schwab has long been a consolidated brokerage giant. The group controls numerous companies active in the most varied financial sectors, market makers, distributors of investment funds (one of the pillars of its success), fiduciary companies and more. The strategy is to act as a high-end discount broker, with higher-than-average commissions but with a very wide range of services, comparable to that of the so-called traditional full-service brokers. Compared to other online brokers, then, it makes an unprecedented choice: it offers free educational courses via the Internet on the use of technology.

Among the strengths, as mentioned, the Mutual Fund Marketplace, a portal for choosing and comparing own mutual funds and other companies; it will then be flanked by the Mutual Fund OneSource, in which the online offer of funds without subscription fees (no load) is concentrated. Focusing above all on asset management, both based on personal advice and on telematic tools, Schwab develops a series of sophisticated applications for portfolio management (Asset Allocation Toolkit, Market Buzz and others). 1996 is also the year of the first Internet market placement. The push comes from private companies that, in order to go public without paying the exorbitant costs of intermediaries specialized in this type of operation, decide to exploit the possibilities provided by the Web. The first, in particular, is Street Spring Brewing, a small American brewer, which at the beginning of 1996 decided to sell its shares during the placement phase also through the unregulated platform Wit-Trade, founded by Andrew Klein, thus managing to raise 1.6 million dollars out of the 5 million total requested from the market. Wit-Trade is a BBS (bulletin board system) similar to that of the more famous Pink Sheet, which shows only buying and selling prices, the latest transactions and contracts relating to the transaction itself. The novelty displaces the SEC, which intervenes and asks Street Spring to suspend the operation to evaluate it. Finally, on April 17, 1996, the SEC, through what in the USA is defined a "no-action letter" (i.e., declaration of non-intervention), limits itself to indicating to Wit-Trade some operational adjustments, implicitly allowing the continuation of the activities without forcing the company to request a specific authorization such as a stock exchange, intermediary, clearing company or other.

It should be emphasized that the SEC, among the arguments contained in the letter, states that "innovation and creativity are the characteristics of the financial markets of our nation that have contributed enormously to a greater efficiency of the capital formation system around the world" : how much irony in these words, thinking back to the events of recent years, from subprime to Enron, from Worldcomm to Bernard Madoff, from speculative activity to conflicts of interest of large banks and rating companies to maxi-bonuses. Despite the approval of the SEC, Klein in 1997 transformed WitTrader into an authorized intermediary. However, the SEC's no-action letter gives way to a large number of automated trading systems, starting with those of the Real Goods Trading Corporation (RGTC), PerfectData, Direct Stock Market and Peoples Stock Network, from which a range will emerge. of professional platforms and technological solutions that will quickly pour into private services. We have therefore arrived on the eve of the great boom of 1997, the year that will mark the moment of transformation of online trading from a niche tool to a mass phenomenon. An explosion of interest that will collide head-on with the stock market crash of March 2000 due to the so-called bursting of the Internet bubble or of the "dot.com"; but until then, online trading will live its golden age.

1997-1999
Online trading takes off in the USA
First online broker in Asia

Since 1997 it has become increasingly difficult to keep track of new companies and new services. The phenomenon of online trading is a consolidated commercial and financial reality that in a few years will bring a quarter of the orders on the stock exchange made online by individuals to the USA. And without forgetting that for at least three years also in Europe (in Italy since the end of 1994), albeit with somewhat different characteristics, the electronic trading of financial securities is a niche in constant expansion. In Asia, the first online broker for individuals appears in 1997.
But what does the strong growth that begins this year come from? The answer is contained in the previous chapters: a group of pioneers makes their previous experience their own and throws themselves over the Web, just as the computerization of the average user intensifies and services, not just financial, multiply. It is, therefore, once again a story of convergence. Convergence between supply, demand, and technology, expertly blended with innovative ideas and entrepreneurial courage.
It is therefore time to give some numbers. According to Fortune magazine, which cites a study by Forrester Research, in April 1995 there are about 400,000 investors in

the United States "placing orders in cyberspace, many using the big three online services America On Line, CompuServe and Prodigy other proprietary non net-worked services, such as Schwab's StreetSmart".

A number that at the end of 1997, according to some estimates, would have reached 2.9 million, 5.3 million at the end of '98 (Forrester Research) and 8.4 million at the end of '99, i.e., at the end of the period taken considered in this first volume.

A "cake" that a few "hungry" people initially share in the United States. In this regard, the aforementioned analysis carried out in 2000 by Kenneth J. Michal for the American Association of Individual Investors (AAII) is interesting, according to which there are 6 online brokers in 1991, 7 in 1994 and all up to now connected direct via modem (dial-up), i.e., not connected to the Internet. Only in 1995 out of 12 companies one offered its service through the Web.

A dozen, which practically means a doubling, a trend that from this moment will be confirmed at least until

1999. Of the 20 brokers active in 1996, 5 are via the Internet while, as said, 1997 is confirmed as the boom year: on the Web there are as many as 25 of the 33 active companies and globally about 153,000 performed online by individuals per day. Progressively everyone is adapting to the new powerful communication channel and in 2000 there will be none of the 76 US online brokers out of the Net. Only the bursting of the bubble in March 2000 will lead to a drastic downsizing of the online financial trading market, so much so that in the 2004 only 54 companies will be active.

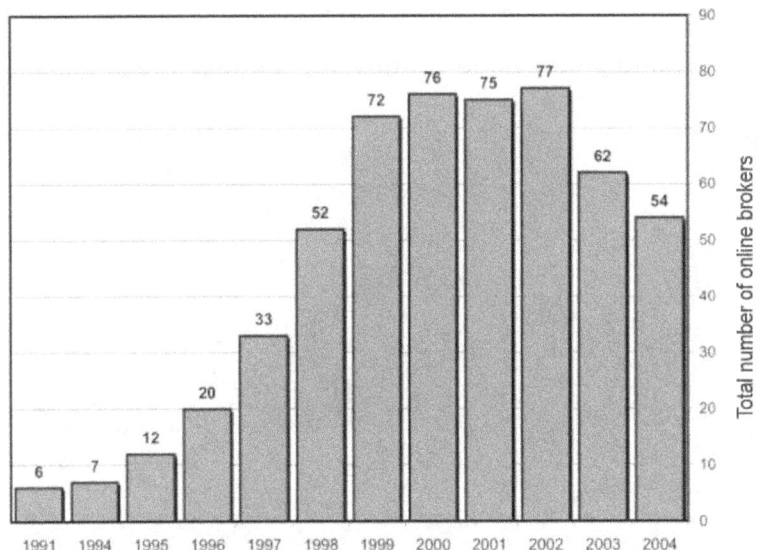

Figure 19 • The growth of online brokers in the United States according to the AAII report. Since 1999, all companies have offered services through the World Wide Web only

Also, according to Forrester Research, in 1996 the online volumes of shares and funds amounted to just over 110 billion dollars, which in 1997 became almost 200 and then grow by 70-80 billion in the following years.

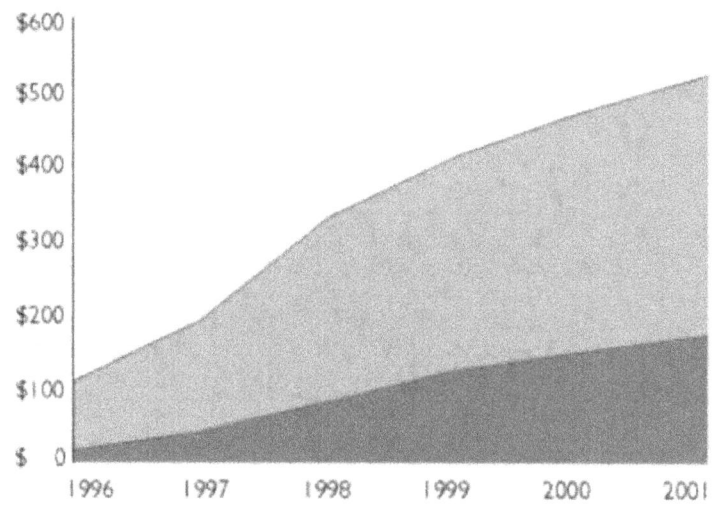

(miliardi)	1996	1997	1998	1999	2000	2001
	94.7	150.9	248.3	289.7	324.6	350.8
	16.7	41.9	82.8	124.3	149.4	173.5
	$111.4	$192.8	$331.1	$414.0	$474.0	$524.3

Source: Forrester Research, Inc.

Figure 20 • Investments made with telematic systems in the United States from 1996 to 2001

In 1996, 1998 and 1999 the main market shares of North American brokers are as follows:
- Charles Schwab 33%, 32% and 28%
- E*Trade 15%, 12% and 12%
- Fidelity 13%, 8% and 10%
- Datek 7%, 7% and 10%

which means that in the boom years the first four brokers take home 60-70% of clients and volumes. The market, in fact, expanding in the number of brokers, clients, trades and volumes proportionally reduces the weight of almost all the largest at the expense of new entrants, who however individually fail to carve out a truly significant share in just three years.

In May 2000 the US General Accounting Office, in a report on online trading delivered to Congress, takes into consideration the data provided by 12 anonymous online brokers, however reporting as these, while representing "less than 10% of the active companies in the sector" (about 160 at the time), collected about 90% of total online volumes in 1999, with about 500,000 executed per day and that, overall, the US market in 1999 collected more or less 10.5 million accounts. Mind-boggling numbers? Perhaps. But to downsize at least as far as real operations are concerned: according to a report drawn up by the SEC on 25 April 2000, the number of private day traders, which represent a "new phenomenon" for the same entity, is no more than 7,000, especially when compared with an estimated 80 million Americans who in 1999 own shares in listed companies and with the 5 million who in total use the Internet to trade them. A few thousand super-active traders, therefore, who according to the SEC in 2000 could move about 15% of the volumes of the NASDAQ. As for possible scammers, in the same year the SEC concludes that, after thoroughly analyzing 22 online brokers, there are no reasons for concern and that the few irregularities found are venial and the result of incorrect interpretations of the regulations at the administrative level.

Another interesting analysis of the AAII concerns the comparison between the first two of the class, namely

Charles Schwab and E*Trade, the results of which can be viewed in the two graphs in Figures 22 and 23. As can be seen, the Schwab dimensions are of some larger size, if only for the fact that it is a company that has been active for decades with a solid base of hundreds of offices around the country, compared to an (almost) new company with innovative technology and a practically unique service.

However, the results can be seen from the evolution over time: Schwab's quarterly net profit is cyclical but within a continuously growing trend, while E*Trade, starting from autumn 2008, goes into the red even with revenues in moderate growth.

And even in the growth in the number of customers there is no competition: between 1997 and 1998 Schwab earned 1.4 million, going from 780,000 to 2.2 million, against the "only" 550,000 of E*Trade, which saw the accounts touch quota 680,000 from the initial 145,000. A more significant percentage growth, without a doubt. But, as you know, it is not with the percentages that you make a turnover. In short, at least for the first few years, traditional business made hybrid by integration with a robust IT infrastructure seems to be the winning model.

Parallel to the growth of competition and the rush to grab digitized customers, commissions plummet according to a curve that, in the case of the most aggressive discount brokers, will come close to 1 or 2 dollars per order in the early years of the third millennium. However, the average will remain around $20 for a long time.

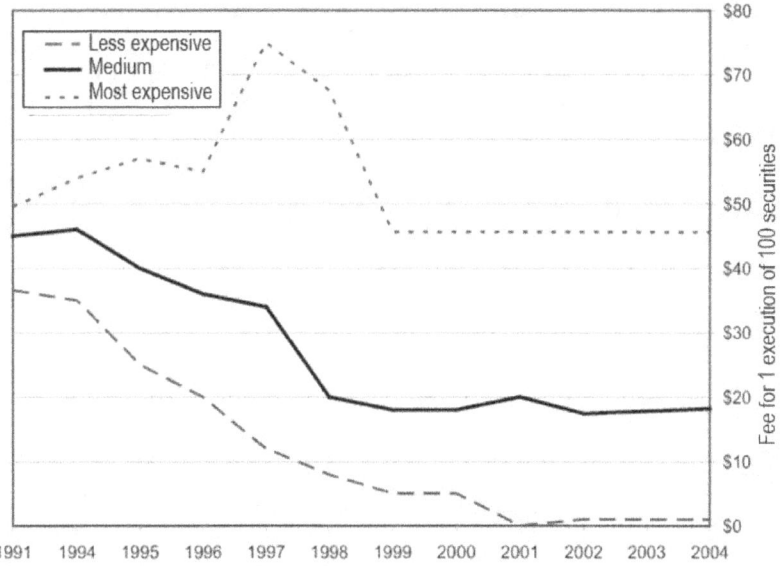

Figure 21 • The curve of the fees per execution of US brokers in the 1990s and at the beginning of the third millennium

As the new millennium opens and the new markets collapse following the bursting of the tech bubble, the online trading industry will once again be dramatically challenged. However, the foundations laid during the 1990s will allow the stability of the most solid brokers and a substantial continuation of the activity that will see new areas of development.

APPENDIX

Sources and bibliography

Andrea Fiorini's book and works:

"Trading and investments online", 2020, Ed. Hoepli (in Italian, also ebook).

"Italian Online Trading Yearbook ", 2014, 2015, 2016, 2017, 2018, 2019, Ed. Mediosfera; 2020-21 Ed. Trading Library (in Italian).

"Trading Online for Dummies ", 1st ed. 2016, 2nd edition 2020, Ed. Hoepli (in Italian, also ebook).

"Investire con il crowdfunding for Dummies", 2021, Ed. Hoepli (in Italian, also ebook).

Articles published in the financial weekly "Borsa&Finanza", 1999-2012, Editori PerlaFinanza (in Italian).

Andrea Fiorini, "Soldi sul filo", 2001, Ed. Hops-Tecniche Nuove (in Italian).

Others sources:

Howard M. Friedman, 2004, "Securities regulation in cyberspace", Aspen Publishers.

Alfred L. Norman, 2009, "Informational Society Online," University of Texas at Austin.

Alfred L. Norman, 2009, "Initial impact of computers in the 60s and 70s", University of Texas at Austin.

Sam Allis et al, "The MIT 150: 150 Ideas, Inventions, and Innovators that Helped Shape Our World", 2011, The Boston Globe.

"Notice of Commission views on computer brokerage system", SEC release no. 34-21383, 9/10/1984.

James W. Cortada, The digital hand, Vol. 2, 2006, Oxford University Press [Cincinnati Stock Exchange].

Anna Ponziani and others, "E-retail finance report in Italy" (half-yearly), 2000-2008, KPMG Advisory (in Italian).

Various authors, "Reference for business", 2011, Advameg.

Dean Furbush, "Program trading and price movement: evidence from the October 1987 market crash", 1989, Financial Management.

"See day traders working hard to influence how the profession is to be defined", 1999, Securities Week (McGraw-Hill).

ICI and SIA, "Equity ownership in America", 1999, Bank.

Jean-Michel Sahut, "On-line brokerage in Europe: actors & strategies", 2003, Array Development.

Niko Marcel Waesche, "Internet entrepreneurship in Europe", 2003, Elgar Publishing.

Marco de Marco, "The virtual bank in Germany", Beltel, December 1997.

JW Smith, JP Selway III, DT McCormick, "The Nasdaq stock market", 1998, NASD.

http://www.nasdaq.com/newsroom/presskit/timeline.stm, 2011, Nasdaq Omx Group.

Bulletin n ° 348, July-August 2000, Commission des Opérations de Bourse (COB), Paris.

Bruno Dranesas, "La voie est libre en France pour la banque sans guichets", 18/1/1995, "Liberation" (in french).

Daniel Fortin, "La banque directe demarre en flanant", 20/03/1995, L'Expansion (in French).

Wikipedia, http://it.wikipedia.org, http://en.wikipedia.org, http://fr.wikipedia.org, http://www.fundinguniverse.com, 2006, The Gale Group.

"Trading On The Computer", June 1, 1984, Inc. Magazine (USA).

Natalie Stetz Tobias, "The meteoric history of online stock trading", 2010, Stock Trading Warrior.

Presidency of the Council of Ministers, 2011, http://www.government.it

"System [AutEx] is planned for block trading", 26/6/1968, "New York Times".

"Boston firm [AutEx] unveils information network for big stock trades", 6/26/1968, "The Wall Street Journal".

Frank Durda, "Dual tone multi-frequency (Touch-Tone) reference", 2006, http://nemesis.lonestar.org

"History of online banking", 2011, eHow Demand Media [Security First Nat Bank].

Mary Cronin, "Banking and finance on the Internet", 1997, Wiley [Videotex, birth of home banking].

"French and british slug it out in teletext battle", 27 November 1980, New Scientist [USA, Videotex].

M. Edwards, "Brighter picture is appearing for business Videotex", August 1985, Communications News.

Peter Dickman, Peter G. Neumann and others, "The risks digest Forum on Risks to the Public in Computers and Related Systems", Volume 6, volume 67m, 24 April 1988,

ACM Committee on Computers and Public Policy (GB) [Duca of Edinburgh, Videotex mail infringement].

Frank Muhlberg, "TeamBank General Information", 2011, Bankenvergleich.net (Germany) [NTB].

"Norddeutsche Teilzahlungskreditbank Dr. Ade & Co. AG, Hamburg: Der Mensch als Schnittstelle", September 26, 1975, COMPUTERWOCHE.DE, IDG Business Media Gmbh (Germany) [NTB] (in German).

Verbraucherbank-Kunden schreiben Überweisungen für Bildschirmtext "Mit der Maschinenpistole im Trojanischen Krieg", 12 June 1981, COMPUTERWOCHE.DE, IDG Business Media Gmbh (Germany) [NTB] (in German).

Bernardo Bàtiz-Lazo, "Technological innovation in retail finance: international historical perspectives", 2011, Taylor & Francis [Rabobank, Barclays].

Ian Martin, "Britain's first computer center for banking: what did this building do?", University of Manchester (GB) [Barclays 1955].

John Cowen, "Report of the Electronics Sub-Committee to the Chief Executive Officer," May 9, 1958 [Barclays 1955].

"ERMA and MICR: the origins of electronic banking", 2012, SRI International (USA) [ERMA].

"Computer wartet auf Arbeit: Selbstbedienung zum Nulltarif geplant", June 18, 1976, Computerwoche.de, IDG Business Media Gmbh (Germany) [NTB].

Howard Finberg, "Before the Web, there was Viewtron", 27 October 2003, Poynter (The Poynter Institute, USA).

William W. Streeter, "Adios, Bank One", 2004, ABA Banking Journal, vol. 96 [Bank One].

"The History of JPMorgan Chase & Co. 200 Years of Leadership in Banking", 2008, JPMorgan Chase & Co. [Bank One, Chase Manhattan, Chemical Bank].

"Home banking by computer", March 29, 1983, "New York Times" [Chemical Bank].

"Home finance in an electronic age", September 20, 1982, "Time" [Chemical Bank].

"BofA, Chemical, AT&T and time plan home banking", June 4, 1985, "Los Angeles Times" [Chemical Bank].

Tom Forester, "High-tech society: the story of the information technology revolution", 1987, "MIT Press".

"Touch Tone telephone will help pay your bills", December 5, 1965, "The Palm Beach Post".

JC Westland, THK Clark, 1999, "Global electronic commerce: theory and case studies", "MIT Press" [touch tone trading, DLJ].

"Tymshare Inc.", 2011, Computer History Museum (Mountain View, California).

Stuart L. Mathison, "Telenet inaugurates service", 1975, "ACM Computer Communications Review".

John Markoff, "Stock market bulletin board supplies quotation", April 5, 1982, InfoWorld [Max Ule].

Michael K. Wolensky, "Securities law and the Internet enforcement issues: application of suitability obligations", 1999, Kutak Rock [on SEC "Computer Brokerage Systems", 9 October 1984. Securities Exchange Act Release No. 34-21383].

Tim Metz, "Black Monday: the stock market catastrophe of October 19, 1987".

Joseph Meth, "The October 19, 1987, market crash", October 19, 2011, DailyMarkets.com

Jim Bartimo, "Clients with micros challenge stockbrokers", April 16, 1984, InfoWorld.

Denise Caruso, "Buying stocks on-line", September 1984, InfoWorld.

Gary Meyers, "Here's how to trade stocks on your home computer", February 11, 1985, "Spartanburg Herald-Journal" and "Gainesville Sun" [Hutton and Spear].

Hank Bannister, "Broker show stock services", Mar 18, 1985, InfoWorld [Fidelity, Spear].

NAICO-Net advertisement, July 28, 1986, InfoWorld

Lisa Spiegelman, "PC-based trading brings the stock market home", December 8, 1986, InfoWorld [Fidelity Investor's Express].

C. Jouzaitis, B. Barnhart, "Hope, risk vie in quest for Wealth Unlimited", May 10, 1987, Chicago Tribune [McGivney, NAICO-Net].

B. Grady, M. Goozner, J. O'Brien, "Ties that bind put to test on clients", February 6, 1990, Chicago Tribune [case against Kopko, North American Holding].

Ed Henry, "When your computer is you broker", July 1994, Kiplinger's Personal Finance Magazine.

Udayan Gupta, "Managing Your money with computers", July 1984, Black Enterprise.

Michael Barrier, "Looking to the long term Discount broker Charles R. Schawb", December 1988, Nation's Business.

Fabrizio Bartoloni, "Storia dei computer giapponesi (1956-1997)", 2009, Punto Informatico (in Italian).

Fabrizio Bartoloni, "USSR, una storia di computer (1948-1989)", 2009, Punto Informatico (in Italian).

Marie Marchand, "La grande aventure du Minitel", 1987, Librairie Larousse (in French).

"Introduction to AN I FSQ-7 Combat Direction Central and AN I FSQ-8 Combat Control Central" [SAGE], 1959-65, IBM Military Products Division.

"SAGE's central processing unit: The FSQ-7 (Whirlwind II)", 2005, American Computer Science Association ASCA.net

"For wires and signs", 2006, AICA http://www.museoaica.it [on Tymnet, Uninet, Telenet and European networks].

William Stewart, "Internet history", 2000-2007, LivingInternet.com

Claude Baum, "The system builders: the story of SDC", 1981, SDC [on SAGE].

Rose Aguilar, "CompuServe wants your money", March 26, 1996, CNET News.

"CompuServe brings banks online via alliance with Braun Simmons & Co.", March 26, 1996, PR Newswire.

B. Becker, S. Schulte, M. Wallach, "Securities law and the Internet", 1998, Practicing Law Institute [DLJ Direct].

John Kador, "Charles Schwab: how one company beat Wall Street and reinvented the brokerage industry", 2002, Wiley.

Andrea Carignani, "Trading on-line in Europa", 2003, Università Cattolica di Milano and University of Regensburg [US broker since 1990] (in Italian).

"Default bank brings internet to town", 21 October 1995, Community Investment Network.

Bill Orr, "Community banking on the Internet", 1995, ABA Banking Journal, Vol. 87.

Denise Duclaux, "The call of the Web: should you take the plunge with an Internet home page? And, if so, how?", 1996, ABA Banking Journal, Vol. 88.

Patrick J. Conway, Charles Duncan, "Interview with a banker: the motivations of Apollo Trust", 23 October 1995, Department of Economics University of North Carolina.

Andreas Crede, "Electronic commerce and the banking industry: the requirement and opportunities for new payment systems using the Internet", Science Policy Research Unit University of Sussex.

"SWIFT history", 2011, http://www.swift.com/about_swift/company_information/swift_history.page, SWIFT.

http://www.edibasics.co.uk, 2011, GXS Ltd (GB) [Financial EDI].

George A. Fontanills, "Trade options online", 1999, Wiley (USA) [broker 1994-96, Datek].

Ian Johnston, "The lineup of the on-line services", May 1993, Kiplinger's Personal Finance Magazine [broker 1990-1994].

"Brokerages become first to let investors buy, sell stocks through the Internet", March 12, 1995, "Los Angeles Times" [Net Investors, K. Aufhouser & C.].

James Aley, "How investors can use the Internet sure", April 17, 1995, Fortune Magazine.

"National Discount Brokers Debuts as Exclusive Provider of Discount Brokerage Services for Women's Connection Online", February 19, 1998, BUSINESS WIRE (USA) [National Discount Brokers].

Kenneth J. Michal, "On-line discount brokers", 2001, AAII (USA) [USA broker 1990-94].

Asish Ramchandran, Vijay Gurbaxani, "On-line discount brokerages: E*Trade vs. Charles Schwab", November 1999, Center for Research on Information Technology and Organizations University of California [1995-1996].

Costas Markides and Paul Geroski, "Colonizers and Consolidators: The Two Cultures of Corporate Strategy. A firm can pioneer a market or scale it but not both ", Autumn 2003 n. 32, Strategy-Business.com [Net Investors, Security APL].

Giancarlo Livraghi, "Dati e statistiche su Internet in Italia, in Europa e nel mondo", 2011, http://gandalf.it [data about Internet] (in Italian).

"Checkfree Corporation completes acquisition of Security APL", May 9, 1996, SEC (http://www.secinfo.com/dsVS7.92G5.c.htm).

"Jack White & Company", 1998, Microsoft Corporation case study for Windows NT.

Mentioned companies

A
Accutrade
Acument Securities...
All American Brokers
Amen & Associates
American Association of Individual Investors (AAII)
American Express...
American Stocks Exchange
America On Line (AOL)
ARPA
Atanasoff Berry Computer
Aufhauser Securities
AuteEx Service Corporation

B
Banc One
Bank of America
Bank of Delaware
Bank of Montreal
Bank of Scotland
Bank One
Barclays
BBC

Borsa Italiana
Brown&Co.
Bunker Ramo
Butler America
Butler

C
Capital Institutional Services
CBS
Charles Schwab & Co.
Chase Manhattan Bank
Checkfree Corp.
Chemical Bank
Chevy Chase Bank
Chicago Mercantile Exchange (CME)
Chi-X
Cincinnati Stock Exchange
Citibank
Committee of London Clearing Bankers (CLCB)
Commodore
CompuTEL Securities
ComputerServe

Consiglio Europeo delle
Ricerche Nucleari
(CERN)
Credit Agricole
Credit Suisse

D
Dahlman Rose & Co.
D`Ancona & Pflaum
DARPA
Deutsche Bank
Deutsche Bundespost
Direct Stock Market
Donaldson Lufkin & Jenrette (DLJ)

E
EF Hutton & Co.
EMI Electronics
English Electric
Enron
E*Trade
Execution Services

F
Federal Communications Commission (FCC)
Ferranti
First Omaha Securities
France Telecom
Fujitsu

G
General Electric
Genie
Google
Götabanken
GPO

H
Hamburg Sparkasse
Harrisdirect
Herzog, Heine & Geduld
Hitachi
Honeywell
Hospital Newspapers Group
Howe-Barnes
Hughes Aircraft

I
IBM
Independent Broadcasting Authority (IBA)
Instinet
Institutional Networks
Intermarket Trading Network (ITN)
Investex
Investment Technology Group
ITV

J
Jack White & Co.
Jonathan Alan & Co.
Joseph P. McGivney
JPM Industries
JP Morgan Chase
JP Morgan

K
K. Aufhauser & Co.

L
La Poste
Lehman Brothers
Lloyds Bank
Lombard Institutional Brokerage
London International Financial Futures & Options Exchange (LIFFE)
London Stock Exchange (LSE)
Lycos
Lyons

M
Manufacturers Hanover Bank
Martin Marietta
Matif
Max Ule & Co.
McDonnell Douglas

MCI
MCI Worldcom
Mellon Bank
Merrill Lynch
Merrin Financial
Metropolitan Museum of Art
Microsoft Network
MIT Lincoln Laboratory
Moore School of Engineering
Morgan Stanley
Morningstar
Mydiscountbroker.com

N
NAH
NAICO
NASDAQ
National Provincial Bank
National Stock Exchange (NSX)
Networked System International (NSI)
Networking and World Information
News Corporation
New York Chamber of Commerce
New York Mercantile Exchange (Nymex)
New York Stock Exchange (NYSE)

Noris Bank
Nortel Networks
North American Investment Corp. (NAICO)
North American Ventures
Nottingam Building Society (NBS)
NYSE Euronext

O
OMX
OSI

P
Pacific Brokerage Services (PBS)
Pacific Stock Exchange
PaineWebber Incorporated
Peoples Stock Network
PerfectData
Pershing & Co.
Philadelphia Stocks Exchange
Pizza Hut
Plantagenet Capital
Poste, Téléphone et Télécommunications (PTT)
Putnam

Q
Quick & Reilly

R
Rabobank
RAND (Research and Development)
Raymond James
RCA
Real Goods Trading Corporation (RGTC)
Reuters News
R. J. Forbes
Robinson-Humphrey

S
Salomon Brothers
Scientific Data System (SDS)
Sears
Securities and Exchange Commission (SEC)
Securities APL
Security Pacific Banks
Shearson
Shearson Lehman Hutton
Shields & Company
Singapore International Monetary Exchange (Simex)
SIP
Southeast Banking
Spear Financial Services

Spear Securities
Sprint
St. John's University
Street Spring Brewing
SWIFT (Society for Worldwide Interbank Financial Telecommunication)
System Development Corporation (SDC)

T
TD Ameritrade
TD Bank
TD Waterhouse
Texas Securities
The Gartner Group
Thomson Financial
Thomson Reuters
Titan Values
Toronto-Dominion Bank
Toronto Dominion
TradeCast
Trade*Plus
TRG
Troster Singer
TSB
Tymnet

U
UAS Automation Systems
Uninet
UNIVAC
University of California Los Angeles
University of Delft
Usenet
US General Accounting Office

V
Verbraucherbank
Verizon
Viewdata

W
Wachovia
Wall Street Investor Services
Waterhouse National Bank
Waterhouse Securities
Web Street Securities
Wellington
Western Electric
Westminster Bank
White Discount Securities
Worldcomm

Y
Yahoo

Mentioned people

A
Aiken, Koward
Anderson, C. Derek
Andreessen, Marc
Asimov, Isaac
Atanasoff, John
Aufhauser, Keith R.

B
Ball, George
Baran, Paul
Barners-Lee, Tim
Bartimo, Jim
Behrens, Herbert
Beranek, Leo
Berry, Clifford
Boesky, Ivan
Bolt, Richard
Bradhurst, S.W.
Brennan, Robert E.
Bruk, Isaak
Bunker, George
Bunkji, Okazaki

C
Cailliau, Robert
Carter, Jimmy
Citron, Jeffrey A.

Clark, Theodor H.K
Corso, Philip
Cotsakos, Christos
Cronin, Mary

D
Di Caprio, Leonardo
Donaldson, William
Dreyfus, Philippe

E
Eckert, John

F
Fedida, Samuel
Flowers, T.H.
Fomon, Robert

G
Giscard d'Estaing, Valéry
Giuliani, Rudolf
Gore, Al
Green, Hugh Carleton

H
Hardy, Norm
Hughes, Howard

J
Jobs, Steve

K
Kay, Alan
Klein, Andrew
Kleinrock, Leonard
Koehn, Peter
Kopko, Frederick
Kussmaul, Wes

L
Larkby, Geoff
Lebedev, Sergei
Leibniz, Gottfried
Levine, Dennis
Levine, Joshua
Licklider, Joseph
Lufkin, Dan

M
Madoff, Bernard
Maschler, Sheldon
McCoy, John
Michal, Kenneth J.
Milken, Michael
Moroney, William
Mr. Gold
Mr. Schifreen

N
Newcomb, Bernard
Newman, Robert

Nora, Simon

O
Obama, Barack

P
Kelleher, Denis P.
Pascal, Blaise
Porter, William
Pouchard, Jean-Yves
Pustilnik, Jerome
Pyatt, Barry

R
Ramo, Simon

S
Saburo, Muroga
Scorsese, Martin
Smiley, Richard
Spear, Charles (Chuck)
Spicer, Robert
Stetz Tobias, Natalie

T
Taub, Jack
Tisch, Tom
Turing, Alan
Tymes, LaRoy

U
Ule, Max

V
Valley, George
Van der Poel, W.L.
Von Meister, Bill
Von Neumann, Janos

W

Westland, J. Christopher
Whipple, Jay
White, Thomas
Wozniak, Steve

Z
Zuse, Konrad

Author's biographical note

Andrea Fiorini

Italian journalist focused on online finance and online trading, he has been following the sector since 1999 and is therefore one of the very few Italian journalists who have witnessed all stages of development, from birth to today. He worked for nearly fifteen years as editor of a financial weekly (Borsa&Finanza) and he is author of various successful books and publications on online trading and finance. He collaborates with banks and financial companies and for the organization of financial training and educational event.

LinkedIn: /in/fiorini
E-mail: fiorini@mediosfera.it

www.Mediosfera.it Institutional
www.NuovaEconomia.com News
www.AnnuarioTrading.it Publishing and news
www.Hanrahan.it Poetry and literature

www.ingramcontent.com/pod-product-compliance
Lightning Source LLC
Chambersburg PA
CBHW052320220526
45472CB00001B/208